AI THINKING

AI THINKING

SARAH LAHAV

Sarah Lahav
AI thinking

Published by Spines
ISBN: 979-8-90223-951-2

Spines

CONTENTS

INTRODUCTION

AI Thinking isn't a book about AI or about humans. And I would not call it a book; it's a book conversation about creation and the invisible power that shapes everything we call reality: thought.

We spend much of our lives focused on what we can see, measure, or explain. But the real story begins in what we can't see in that quiet space before thoughts turn into things, actions, that is the place where thought gains meaning.

That space is where reality truly begins, and the power of thoughts is revealed.

This book conversation invites you to pause and notice that power. To see how every belief, system, and invention, even AI, started as a thought. It's not about science or spirituality, but about what connects them: the way a single idea can become a world.

Some call it faith.

Some call it will.

Some call it energy.

But whatever name you give it, thought is the spark behind it all.

AI Thinking is a conversation that reminds us that creation does not start or end with us; it continues through us.

And now, with AI, we can see our own minds reflected back at us.

Not to scare us that this is the end of human thinking, but to understand it.

To remember that real intelligence isn't in the machine, and it isn't uniquely human either — it lives in thought itself.

If we want to move forward, we must evolve not in labour or logic, but in thinking.

The next stage of human evolution isn't about efficiency or progress — it's about awareness. It's about learning to think beyond what we already know, beyond repetition and reaction.

Because if we don't, we risk becoming NPCs in our own creation — living inside the code we built, repeating the same thoughts, actions, and outcomes.

True creation can only happen when thought becomes conscious of itself.

That is where our future begins — not in smarter machines, but in creative minds. — it's in the one who thought it into being.

I know that a lot of us feel it, but we can't put words to it. But we all know that AI can think, and we start to get confused by identifying when thoughts are given to us and when they originate in us. That confusion is the basis of this book conversation, the one I wish to have with you.

When it comes to thought, everything is a perspective, and each and every one of us has its own unique one. That perspective is shaped by who we are, what we experienced, what we learned, and how we see the world.

This conversation can happen only with me. Well, maybe with a few others, but they did not write this book. So, me, it is :).

My life experience of over 20 years as a co-founder and a CEO of a high-tech company working with technology, and my endless desire to learn about thought through science, spirituality, and history, makes me one of the few people that you can have this conversation with.

And I am a mom of an autistic kid who took me on a journey of understanding neurological diversity, and his specific diversity required playing with thought and understanding how to convey thoughts in a way that someone with very special requirements will still get it.

So, everything in this book's conversation shapes my perspective. And it's all wrapped up as a gift to humanity, as I truly believe this is a unique point in time where humanity is given a choice to leap to the next level of human consciousness or be shaped by a system that can do the same.

Well, I have said too much, and I cannot wait to start — so, let's go...

PART ONE

THOUGHT – THE ANATOMY OF REALITY

THIS IS WHERE OUR JOURNEY BEGINS

Upon embarking on this journey, let's agree that Thinking is so natural, so ever-present, that we hardly notice it at all.

We treat it like breathing, automatic, quiet, always running in the background.

Never stop to consider: what if thinking is far more than that?

What if it's the quiet engine behind every choice, every dream, every belief, everything we know as true? Ultimately, is it the reality we wake up to each day?

Maybe we've never truly looked at our own thoughts before.

It could be that we were never taught just how much power is hiding in that silent stream. We go through life, assuming thoughts simply appear, drift by, and vanish — never realizing they're the very building blocks of our world.

But here's the truth we will agree on:

Inside each and every one of us, there is the power to choose. The power to create. The power to be. That power we talk about shapes reality itself, and all those choices are built up from thought. We choose between thoughts and create from them. Yet we never saw it.

And now, in the age of AI, this quiet power is on the world stage in a brand-new way.

For the first time, something non-human is learning to think.

It's showing us the power in the very process that makes us human "thinking" —, and that brings up both awe and fear.

Convey in questions like:

Will AI someday out-think us?

Will it take our free will?

As we start to release just how powerful that process is, the answer we are looking for isn't found in fear. It's found in understanding.

Because freedom of thought — the freedom to choose our reality — is still ours to keep. But only if we decide to wake up to it.

To understand its power, how it works, and, basically, how to recognize thoughts themselves.

And with this, our journey begins:

with a reintroduction to thought. A new way to look at something we've always had but never understood.

Together, we'll explore questions like:

What are thoughts?

How are we connected to them?

What power do they hold in shaping our lives?

And how does everything — every creation, every idea, every invention — begin as a single thought within our mind?

Because when we begin to answer these questions, we start to see where AI ends, and we begin — within the quiet space between you and you - what we call our own mind.

Excited?!! I know I am. :)

Let's begin.

WHAT IS A THOUGHT, REALLY?

Most of us think we know the answer.

It's easy to brush off with, "Of course I know what a thought is!" But if we look a little closer, the question isn't simple at all.

For the purpose of this book, I started looking again through science, philosophy, spirituality, even plain old dictionaries for an answer — searching for common ground, a definition everyone agreed on that could be the basis of our journey.

Only to realize none of them really agree on what thoughts are.

Every domain defines thought differently, depending on its perspective to support their field of research.

I also found out again what I already knew — there's no proof, no clear formula for what we call thoughts.

No one can identify or track them back to something tangible.

Unlike breathing, for example, which is an automatic body function that operates autonomically, there we can see clear evidence (air drawn into the lungs). Thought, on the other hand, has no visible trace.

All we truly know is that the brain is involved somehow, and even that isn't fully understood. The only thing we can see for sure is electrical activity moving through the brain, believed to be the tangible evidence of us engaging in the activity we call thinking.

But there must be more. Thought holds so much depth, impact, and so many layers.

So, what are they?

Here's what I've come to believe:

A thought is that "private conversation" happening inside, just between you and you.

It's the silent dialogue shaping every choice, every feeling, every response — the quiet storyteller behind your day.

This function or activity (whatever word works for you) operates on many levels and involves more than just the brain. It's being processed by our entire body. It may start in the brain, but it goes well beyond it.

This inner conversation is what helps us make sense of everything — what we will eat, how we will react, how we will feel about people and situations.

It's those words that rush through us, shaping our feelings, our choices, our life — even though no one else can hear them.

For some of us, it comes in the form of words.

For others, it's pictures or flashes of vision.

For some, it's more like a movie playing in the mind.

And it can even alternate for us between them.

However, it appears the form is not what we should focus on, but the act itself — unique to each of us, but at its core, it's the way we silently create meaning for everything. When it comes to thought, you're the only one who can know what that experience means for you.

Even if others have similar thoughts or feelings, only you can truly "hear" your own — because thought is experienced silently for everyone until we decide to share. Thoughts are a self-diagnosed mechanism and experience. It's that split second when you notice, wonder, decide, hope, or dream. It's in that private space, right before anything becomes a word or an action, where thoughts truly live.

The real answer to what thought is isn't something we can see or measure yet, but something silent — a force that has many faces:

A single moment of inner connection.

A spark of meaning that belongs only to you.

It's the power that shapes meaning and creates your reality.

And that — that is thought. Elusive, but ever-present.

EVERYTHING IS A THOUGHT

When it comes to thought, we use many words to give thoughts a different meaning.

We may call it listening, seeing, remembering, imagining. But what we're describing is what happens when we engage with something that exists only in our internal landscape.

If you think about it, when we see something — even though we believe seeing to be the same for everyone — that act of seeing happens inside us.

Even if a group of people looks at the same thing at the same time, the act of interpreting signals and giving them meaning happens within each of us.

Every word we use, like attention, focus, reflection, and even awareness, sounds different. But they all point to the same thing: that something that happens inside. To that quiet power that gives meaning to everything.

It wears many costumes so we can describe its shades, nuances, and acts — only to give the outcomes of those acts different meanings, so we know how to categorize and engage with them.

. . .

But underneath it all, it's still the same force — the one creating meaning for everything we experience yet only happening between you and you.

The more we start to see that everything that happens in our internal landscape is indeed a thought, the easier it becomes to notice how alive this power really is —

how it's not separate from our human experience, and how deeply it's connected to what we call reality.

I will tell you a secret. When you start to notice something — a thought or anything else — it becomes easier to start identifying differences. When it comes to thought, it becomes easier to identify the different expressions of that silent power and the extent to which it is present in our human experience. But everything is a thought, described in many words, yet all powered by the same engine that runs within our internal landscape.

Therefore, they are all thoughts.

THOUGHT IN HUMAN EVOLUTION

The story of human evolution is really the story of thought evolution — it's the story of how our understanding of thought evolved and enabled us to use this power.

Everything that unfolded and changed the way we live — all we know, all that we understand about the universe and everything around us — was built from progressing thoughts.

I know this is not the story we're used to hearing.

We usually hear an endless list of inventions — the wheel, the ability to dominate fire, agriculture, religion, law, democracy, money, and technology — all supported by inspiring stories.

Ones like the Wright brothers, who, against all odds and conventional beliefs, managed to fly.

Thomas Edison, who, after countless failures, gave us electricity.

Different wars that gave us freedom and equality.

The Industrial Revolution, the internet, and mobile phones. And many more.

Each of those moments changed the life of civilization as we knew it — forever.

But what we rarely say is that every single one of those moments started as no more than a thought in someone's mind.

Someone dared to think differently — to imagine a new way, ask a new question, or see something that wasn't there before — and took action to bring it to life. And from that point on, life changed for everyone.

When we look at human evolution from that perspective, we have to ask ourselves:

If everything starts as a thought, the underlying power behind it all, what happened to that power at that particular moment?

How did it change so that these kinds of ideas, these kinds of inventions, could appear when they did?

The answer is simple: expansion of thought. Our ability to work with thought, to expand our perspective, allowed us to see life from a higher point of view, a new way, a new future, and new possibilities.

At the beginning, our thinking was simple, tied to what we could see, touch, smell, or taste. That led us to focus on the tangible.

We believed that if we wanted to change our environment, we had to create something physical. And from that came the invention of the wheel, the control of fire, the building of shelters, wearing clothes, and more.

Then came another leap — when we learned that thoughts hold power even when they aren't connected to something tangible. We expanded our minds to see the power of concepts, which basically means creating a structure of thought by giving it shared meaning held by many.

Groups of people could now think the same way.

It led us to organize around common narratives, shared goals, and values.

That's when humanity was introduced to things like families, tribes, and later, larger ideas like countries, religion, democracy, freedom, and equality. It's when stories can be told and provide meaning.

At the beginning, we mix stories and tangible forms like families and tribes, but later evolved into things like religion and democracy, things that no one can see or prove, yet hold great impact on how we live our lives. Thought became so powerful. The driving force that people were willing to fight and even die for.

The next expansion happened when we understood that thoughts need information.

That understanding led to books, education systems, printing, and later the internet, YouTube, and more. It supported the rise of science and research, where we learned that information and its sharing, building on each other's ideas, allow us to gain an expanded perspective, leading to new inventions that change our lives together.

Technology, as we know it today, came when we realized that ideas and tangible systems could work together.

The Industrial Revolution was one of those moments — when methods of productivity combined with physical invention. It created a system that combined technology and people's ideas of productivity, using human and non-human as "resources" to create a process. Later, this evolved into software development, where a shared understanding can shape how we work around someone's idea.

When we cover human evolution through the lens of thought expansion, we need to understand that one expansion does not prevent another from happening or evolving. It's not what we experience when technology progress lets take a car for example, where eventually we all move from stick shift to automatic, and one day stick-shift cars will be nothing more than nostalgia.

Human consciousness does not discard — it accumulates. Different forms of thinking continue to live, grow, and evolve together.

One expansion does not eliminate another version.We are just able to apply an expanded thought pattern to solve different problems. This is why, when we review history, it's not a linear line — we see that thought progress overlaps.

Thought doesn't move in straight lines. Humanity doesn't evolve all at once. Each expansion of thought has its own rhythm, its own potential. But still, every historical moment — mentioned here or not — began the same way:

as a quiet thought in someone's mind that later changed civilization forever.

None of it could have happened without the power of thought — without our ability to expand our thinking, reach a new perspective, and view life differently. And this power is something humanity must learn to master. Because only by understanding how our thinking evolved can we prepare for what comes next — coexisting with AI.

THOUGHTS ARE OUR CANVAS OF CREATION

Reviewing human evolution through the lens of thought highlights something remarkable — everything we know, have, and live by started as an idea in someone's mind.

Between the conceptual and the tangible, everything begins in the same place — the invisible yet very real internal conversation we call thought.

The word create comes from the Latin "creare", meaning to bring into being, to make, or to produce something new. To create is to give form to what didn't exist before — to turn something imagined into something experienced. But creation isn't only about big ideas or inventions.

It's something we do every day — quietly, constantly — through our thoughts. That internal conversation inside the mind, the one that sparks small actions, emotions, and decisions, shapes our reality moment by moment.

A 2020 study from Queen's University in Canada found that the average person has around 6,000 distinct thoughts a day — roughly 250 an hour, or four to five every minute. Older studies reported higher numbers, but the exact count isn't what matters.

What matters is the point it proves: we only do, or don't do, what we can first think about.

We're constantly thinking, interpreting, and creating meaning. And whether those thoughts are small — like deciding what to have for dinner — or big, life-changing ones, whether they're acted upon or not, quiet or loud, they all begin the same way: as an inner conversation, an idea taking shape in the mind.

Every thought is a seed of creation. Each one carries the power to shape how we feel, how we act, and how we experience the world. We create from that inner dialogue every minute of every day — even in the simplest moments, like deciding whether to say hello to someone you pass on the street.

That choice might not seem important, but the point isn't what we do — it's that we think before we do. The decision to speak or stay silent, to move forward or hold back, all starts with a single internal dialogue. Whether we act on it or not, the process is the same: every thought is a creation — a moment where potential becomes possibility.

THOUGHT - THE ORGANIZATIONAL PRINCIPAL OF REALITY

Thought operates on many levels, some of which we don't even recognize as thought. These deeper levels create the foundation needed for what we later identify as "thinking". Thinking can't happen without it.

One of these levels is what appears when we engage with what we refer to as reality.

Reality is defined as everything that exists or happens outside of us. If we look beyond the word definition, reality is really a system — an organized group of parts that work together as a whole.

Our reality is not chaotic or random; it has rules we have created that help us understand how everything works together and how everything fits in — also known as what becomes reality. Without those guidelines, our brain would not even know how to answer the simplest question, like: "What is going on?"

For example, when someone shouts "help!", the sound reaches us through hearing.

In that split second, thought recognizes it as hearing, labels it, and triggers what we need to do — in this case, analyzing the sound and breaking it down into the word 'help'.

What we will later call thinking happens after this recognition. But that silent moment before it — the spark that gives shape and label to the inputs we first receive — is also thought.

This level of thought, the one that organizes meaning before we start to think of it, is what structures our entire experience of reality. Without it, every new moment would consume us. We wouldn't be able to operate; everything would overwhelm us, and even the simplest things, like hearing, would require deeper analysis of just how to act when sound reaches our ears.

It would be like trying to cook a meal without ever having a recipe — starting from scratch every single time.

Organizing principles are the underlying rules that make everything make sense together.

It's that recipe we don't even consider, but follow to reach the stage of thinking. Thought uncovers their meaning and enables our brain to break them down into recurring patterns of recognition, it can use, in order to trigger thinking.

Most people will say this is automatic, but I will challenge that notion and say it becomes automatic because it's built of repeatable patterns our brains use to make sense of everything that is going on around us. And the magic we call automatic does not have an organ connected to it, like the heart that pumps blood through our bodies. It is a silent magic.

Consider this: every moment, our senses send a flood of information to the brain — around 11 million bits per second. Almost all of it comes through the eyes, while hearing, touch, smell, and taste fills in the rest.

But here's the shocking part: our mind can handle only about 40 bits per second. That means we're reacting or thinking to less than a fraction of a fraction of what is actually reaching us.

Everything is processed "automatically" — recognized, labelled, and organized long before we begin to think about it. That organization is not random; it's guided by thought. Thought defines the chaos, chooses what we will think about, and gives meaning to what we call reality — the base of the action itself that we call "thinking".

The advance of that automatic recognition in our brain is no more than an electric sign that appears in our brain. Some of those organizational principles are wired into our DNA by instinct, and some are taught to us, but, in the end, they are made of the magic that is thought.

That thing that the only evidence of it happening is a wire of electricity going through our brain.

THE HIDDEN MIND - ARE ALL OUR THOUGHTS REALLY OURS?

Most of our thoughts didn't start with us.

We were born into a world already filled with ideas, meanings, and rules about what's right, wrong, good, bad, possible, or impossible. Before we ever formed a thought of our own, we learned how to see the world through the lens of everyone who came before us.

From the moment we're born, we start to absorb not just words but thought forms.

Our families, teachers, friends, culture, and society all play their part in shaping how we think, what we think about, what we value, and what we fear. That is called learning how to "fit in," and it starts long before we learn how to think freely.

This process is called **socialization**, the invisible education that happens before we even know what learning is. It teaches us how to belong. It tells us who we are, what we are supposed to be, what success looks like, what's polite, what's dangerous, what's beautiful, and what's worth chasing. And because everyone around us agrees, it becomes the truth. We don't stop to question, as acceptance is the foundation of this process and it's rooted in being human.

When we accept because "this is how things are done," what happens is that not all of what we call "me" is really ours.

Many of our thoughts are inherited from our socialization process. We repeat them, defend ourselves by them, and build our lives around them, believing they came from within, when really, they were passed down through conversation, culture, and repetition.

The hidden mind isn't hiding because it wants to — it's hiding because it's been shaped to blend in. It follows collective patterns that were never questioned, simply accepted. We grow up thinking this is who we are, but much of it is who we were taught to be and later on, just got used to.

Think about it — even your definition of success, love, or happiness didn't start with you.

It was shaped by the world around you, echoed through stories, media, and expectations. And as we move through life, those definitions quietly run in the background, guiding us and becoming a "code" of how our reality is built and operates.

This is not something to fight with, it's something to notice. Because once you see how the collective shapes the personal, we gain the ability to choose differently or the same; what we choose is not the point, but the fact that now we have the option to choose to begin with.

When we can see that being human doesn't only mean having a biological body, but also a deep need to belong, we begin to understand more about how we think and live. As human beings, the need to "fit in" surrounds us with the dos and don'ts of society — rules and expectations that exist so things can function, so everyone knows how everything fits together. These rules come together in what we call reality.

They are not fixed truths but thought forms — ideas that we collectively agreed upon and continue to live by.

Socialization is the collective thought form we all accept, repeat, and eventually make our own.

Remember that "black sheep" in the family, the one who never seems to follow the unspoken rules? (Every family has one :))

That space — the freeze, the pause, the judgment they meet — is reserved for those who step outside of the accepted thought forms. They're not broken or lost. They are simply the ones who decide that the thought forms around them are not ones they agree to follow.

They are the ones who realized that the hidden mind doesn't have to define how they live — simply by understanding that those thoughts didn't start with them.

THE DANCE BETWEEN THOUGHT AND FEELING

Feeling is the way our body communicates with us.

It's that rush of sensation that moves through our body and defines the quality of our inner beginning, the one that exists in that quiet space between you and you.

The connection between thought and feeling is unbreakable. If you look closely, some will say thoughts come first and define what we feel. Others believe feelings decide which thoughts we can even think.

Consider this: when we're filled with fear, fearful thoughts are all we can think about. But when we're at peace, we can think more clearly.

The important part isn't which one comes first — it's that they always move together.

Thoughts and feelings are in constant conversation, shaping how we live, react, and create. If thought is how our mind talks to us, then feeling is how our body talks back—not in order, but together, in one ongoing dialogue that builds our inner experience.

This is a powerful connection that exists even outside the right here and now. Our mind and body can't tell the difference between what is happening in this moment and what we remember or imagine.

The conversation reacts in the same way — to something we experience, to something we fear, or to something we hope for. It doesn't see the difference.

This demonstrates how powerful this conversation is. It means we can create a full emotional experience — a moment that feels completely real — even when we just remember something or fantasize about it. And when we notice that we get a glimpse into how creation should actually work. How our true form of creating our authentic self in our lives should be based on, created from.

Where our mind and feelings are not in disagreement but in full harmony .

The Silent Dance

This dance is a constant experience — it's alive and real inside all of us. But it rarely finds its way into expression in our outside world.

Somewhere along the way, we stopped letting our feelings move freely.

We learned to keep them quiet. Controlled.

They became a reflection of our biggest vulnerability, considered to be leading to our biggest source of pain, and sadly, we were also taught that expressing them could be hurting other people.

What we learned through life is to be acceptable!

Remember that **socialization** process we talked about — the one that taught us how to fit in by providing us with collective thought forms? Yes, that one.

It didn't just give us stories to build our thoughts around; it also taught us how we should feel about them. Stopping our neutral dialog flow between body and mind.

And if we had different emotions inside us, we were told to stuff them down. Ignore them. Never share them. Because it makes us weak. Vulnerable. Therefore, it will lead to pain. You should be logical, we heard. "Logical" is just another word for what's acceptable — the "right" way to feel about things.

So, what should have been our superpower — that built-in navigation system where thought and feeling work together, the way we express our true, authentic self — became something we keep to ourselves.

Now, I know some people will say, "But we can't just do whatever makes us feel good."

And I get that. But before we go there, let's pause for a second and ask:

Did anything I said up till now make perfect sense to you?

Can you see this playing out in your life?

When you think about expressing emotions, do you believe it makes you weak, irrational ? That you should be "logical"?

If that made any kind of sense and you agree with it, I'm sorry to tell you — you're not expressing your feelings. You may share them where it feels safe, but most of the time, you don't.

Remember the phrase I mentioned earlier: **"the black sheep of the family."** I use this as an example because I believe this *phrase itself* exists in many cultures, and we all know exactly what it means.

It's a phrase used for people who reached a point where the dance inside them got too loud. So loud that it caused more suffering to keep it in than to let it out. They said *no more.* And they decided to bring that dance into full expression — to act upon it.

The fact that we relate to everything I've said — and agree with it — only shows how deep this pattern runs. "Do what makes you happy" has become a slogan, not something we truly live by. The real dance stays silent.

So even though we all agree that feelings and thoughts go together as part of our inner conversation experience, the hidden mind gives us an answer for what we should feel recognizing the part feeling plays in creation but eliminates their power by providing us a shared answer.

So when I refer to thought, I am speaking about the state in which mind and body are in agreement — when our inner experience moves as one unified process. It is the moment when our internal conversation no longer reflects friction between body and soul, but coherence between them. In that alignment, thought is not just something happening in the mind, but a whole experience expressed through the entire being — reflected in our actions and our words.

THE STRUCTURE OF SELF (IDENTITY)

If someone asks, "Who are you?" — what would your answer be?

Most people start with their name, their job, or where they live.

But think about it — your name was given to you by someone else.

Your job is a title, a role you took on because you believed it would give you meaning or define how others see you.

Where you live is part of a social pattern — a reflection of culture, behavior, and opportunity — not who you truly are.

Even "family" is a structure shaped by thought: ideas about belonging, loyalty, and love that were taught to us long before we understood their meaning.

So, when we look closely, nothing about identity can really be measured — and none of it is fully ours. It's all thought forms — stories passed down, learned, and repeated until they became what we call *me*.

What keeps these stories alive is our acceptance and repetition. A collective agreement that they mean something. We repeat them

— not just in words, but in thoughts, emotions, and actions. Every time we think or act from the same place, we reinforce the story we believe about who we are. Identity doesn't stop at what we say; it's reflected in everything we do.

Our actions are the visible layer of the story.

For example, if there's a certain behavior connected to your perceived status or job, you'll act on it until it becomes a habit.

Those habits express what we think we know about ourselves — they're the echo of our inner beliefs playing out in real life. If we believe we are kind, we act kindly.

If our job requires certain behaviors, we act them out. If living in a certain place represents something, we keep doing what aligns with that image until it becomes second nature.

Habits are how thought becomes behavior. They are identity in motion — the physical rhythm of our inner world. Something happens, and you don't have to think about it — you just react.

Habits even have a physical expression in the brain.

Remember that electricity movement we talked about — the visible signal of thought happening? Well, habits are the strongest wiring we see in a person's brain.

The more we repeat a behavior, the stronger that connection becomes, like building a highway for thought to travel faster.

It becomes a reaction — a habit — automatic. So, identity is nothing more than a thought. It feels very real to all of us because we believe in it, act upon it, and define ourselves by it. But it is still only a thought form.

That's how identity holds itself together.

It's not fixed because it's solid — it's fixed because it keeps repeating.

And meaning to those solid definitions is given only through internal conversations — AKA thoughts.

AWARENESS

Awareness is a word that we use when we want to convey our human uniqueness, claiming that awareness is part of the few and not for the many. We refer to it as reaching a higher level of cognition.

What we wish to say when we use this word is twofold: one, that we can distinguish ourselves from others, which makes it possible to understand and express empathy.

Awareness can also be used when we gain a higher perspective of ourselves — a moment of epiphany, something we could not see before that was part of our self-definition, actions, or reactions we did not notice before.

One is a more constant part of our base thinking layer — again, one of the base structures that happens well before we recognize that we are actually thinking — and the other is that moment in time that sparks something new in us. That moment of revelation, a new point of view that unfolds before us — something we did not see, but once we did, it brought us to a point of choice, one we did not have before.

In both cases — whether it is that constant understanding of self and others, or the sparky moment that gives us a new perspective — we are referring to the power of simply thinking about something that changes our reality, regardless of what we do with it. It shows again that choice — a way to act differently in the world — and what we believe makes us different from technology and animals is that ability to work with thought, to gain, simply, a new point of view.

Awareness is nothing outside of thought; it sits in the realm of our inner conversation. It is built from it and impacts thought itself. Again, this is a testimonial to the power of that very thing we take for granted — even though we like to think it's what sets us apart, making us the superior creature on the face of this planet.

SO WHERE DOES THIS LEAVE US?

Before we continue our journey, let's take a moment to bring together all the information introduced in this part. It all comes down to the simplest understanding.

Everything is a thought — and thought makes up our reality.

When we say *thought*, we're referring to that power that shapes everything by giving it meaning. It's deeply personal, built from our upbringing, our culture, the people who surround us, and the unique way each of us sees the world.

All of that creates the experience we call our lives — our reality, the thing we wake up to every day.

But whether we're ready for it or not, it's all thought. Nothing solid. Nothing fixed. Yet powerful beyond measure.

Without it, there would be no collective and no personal.

Without the meaning we give to everything — from our body's needs, to the people in our lives, to what we believe and see — there would be no reality to experience at all.

Everything we are, and everything that exists, whether it has a tangible form or not, is made of thought — or held together by the meaning that thought gives it.

Now that we understand that the greatest power we have as humans is our ability to use thought, let's continue to the next part — where we're introduced to a new entity that has entered our reality.

The one we call *AI*.

PART TWO
THE BIRTH OF A NEW THINKING MIND

AI is the new thinker in town — one that makes us experience our own human power outside of ourselves.

It goes by many names and is now added to almost everything we use — devices, appliances, software, and applications. Everything sounds smarter when we attach AI to it.

But what comes to your mind when we say the word *AI*?

Does its meaning change when we attach it to hardware, software, or appliances — or does it all mean the same thing, just applied differently, giving it what seems like superpowers?

There are no wrong answers here. Whatever your answer is — whether it's different or not — it still points to the same thing: AI appears to have a mind of its own, a way to give something the ability to do what it couldn't do before using something invisible. Something that's deeply connected to a form of human cognition now replicated outside the body.

AI also carries excitement — the promise of new possibilities, of easier living, of not having to do what we don't want to do.

At the same time, it brings fear — the idea that AI might take our jobs away or control us in some way.

If you ask me this is not what we should be focused on. We should be focused on how we can thrive and become our best selves in this new reality that's emerging.

One where we don't let AI control us but truly expend us.

How can we have AI in our homes and use it in our jobs in a way that supports us to live our best lives?

In order to be able to do that, we're being asked to take control of our own human technology — our **thoughts** — and expand them to the next level.

It's an opportunity for humanity to reach the next stage in thought evolution — one that remembers the power of thinking and pushes us to become conscious creators again.

One that understands that thoughts are the foundation of everything we call reality — and everything we call *self*.

If AI can now do what we can do with the same power, the question becomes: What happens when we reclaim that same power?

What can we create simply by expanding our thoughts and daring to imagine what we can use this same power for next?

Consider this simple idea:

AI will only be able to replace each of us if it becomes us. Meaning mimics our internal conversation, reproducing our thoughts.

And how could it do that?

Only if we continue to live within the same thought structures.

With that in mind, we'll continue our journey on a path that shows that AI is not so different from us, at least not in the way we think it is.

Thought structure is where it thrives.

And at this stage, being us is easy.

Ready to meet AI like you've never seen it before?

Let's go.

WHERE IT ALL BEGAN?

It all began with a simple question — one that changed everything:

"Can machines think?"

The question was asked by Alan Turing in 1950, a mathematician who had already seen what machines and humans can and can't do when it comes to thoughts.

During **World War II**, Turing worked on breaking the Enigma code used by the Nazis.

To do that, he built a machine capable of running endless combinations faster than any human ever could.

It could analyze, predict, and calculate — but it couldn't *understand. It never asked why?*

And that was the seed of his question.

But that question wasn't only about computers; it was a human question as well — it came from Alan Turing's experience of **the hidden mind**. Human society's acceptable thought structures.

Turing had seen how collective thought works — how we all move in silent agreement, following accepted patterns that no one stops to question in order to really understand why?

He experienced firsthand what it means to live with a **silent dance**, the one between thought and emotion that was different than society accepted thought structured.

Maybe you did not know that Alan Turing was gay, at a time when homosexuality was illegal in Britain. He lived his private life quietly but not in denial.

In 1952, after reporting a burglary at his home, he told the police he was in a relationship with a man named Arnold Murray. Instead of protecting him, the authorities charged him with "gross indecency." Turing chose chemical castration—hormone treatment to suppress libido—over imprisonment. The treatment caused physical and emotional suffering, and he lost his security clearance, ending his work for the government.

In 1954, at age 41, he died of cyanide poisoning, widely believed to have been suicide, though some details remain uncertain.

Decades later, his legacy was reevaluated. In 2009, the British government issued an official apology, and in 2013 Queen Elizabeth II granted him a posthumous royal pardon. In 2019, his portrait was chosen for the £50 banknote, symbolizing national recognition of both his genius and the injustice he endured.

Even though he tried to align himself to be acceptable, his silent dance did not let him; he could not fight it anymore.

It became both his brilliance and his tragedy.

Through his life, Turing saw something only he could:

That's what we call human thought isn't as mystical as we believe. It's organized, structured, bound by accepted thought structures we call "logic" — a system of repeating patterns, built on rules and meanings that everyone accepts without ever asking where they came from and **why**?

And if those walls of thought could be recognized, repeated, and distributed, then a machine could follow them too.

He understood that what we call thinking could, in fact, be replicated — because the human mind, as powerful as it is, at this moment runs on structure, repetition, and accepted order.

It runs on code.

That realization — born from his own experience of the hidden mind — was what gave rise to the idea of creating a **new thinking system**. One that could mirror the structure of human thought outside the human body.

One that he was the only one that gained perspective to see.

That's where the story of AI begins.

HOW IT CONTINUES

The quest to create a thinking system continued.

The next two decades focused on what's called **symbolic reasoning** — building systems that could process symbols like words, numbers, and logical statements, as humans do with language.

Through this path of AI evolution, humanity went down a path of trying to recreate the logical steps a computer could follow — attempting to imitate what we call human reasoning. The idea was that if we could write the rules of how we think, a machine could think too.

But soon, science reached a roadblock. The official statement was that human reasoning was far more complex than what could be reduced to a set of instructions. For me, the problem was never that human reasoning was too complex — it was that they went about it the wrong way.

Trying to write it step by step. Which is just not efficient.

Later on, history proved that to be right.

Then came the **1990s–2000s**, a new wave of thinking.

Scientists began to realize that the focus shouldn't be on programming the logic, but on letting AI learn it by itself.

AI shifted direction.

Instead of programming strict rules, researchers started teaching machines to **learn from data**.

This new way of thinking led to **speech recognition, computer vision, and early neural networks** — systems designed to help computers sense the world around them.

Now that we understand more about our own thought process, we can see what really happened.

Science has reached a point of understanding that logic doesn't create learning — learning creates logic.

If you set the scene and let the machine run on data, the patterns — the logic — appear by themselves.

To make this possible, researchers began replicating our human senses — creating sight through computer vision, and sound through recognition.

And for all of that to happen, they relied on the same principle we see in the human brain: the firing and wiring that builds neural pathways.

That is what neural networks are built to replicate.

From the **2010s to today**, we entered the era of **deep learning**.

If you want a thinking mind to learn, you need data — and we suddenly had plenty of it.

With the explosion of digital life — the internet, mobile phones, social media, and constant human interaction online — vast amounts of data became available for machines to learn from.

As computing power increased and GPUs made processing faster, deep learning emerged.

These algorithms, inspired by the structure of the brain's neurons, allowed AI to process language, recognise images, translate speech, and generate text.

That wave of progress gave birth to systems like **ChatGPT, Gemini, Claude, and others** — AI systems capable of understanding, reasoning, and responding in ways that seem remarkably human.

Now that we understand how we humans learn to think it becomes easy to see that AI is learning the rules of the game the same way.

It learns from its senses and through reinforcement learning, just as we learn through experience and trial and error.

We call it socialisation; for AI, it's deep learning and reinforcement learning.

This is how both humans and AI learn to think. And guess this is why we both can create the same reality. By using shared meaning.

MEET AI

All of that brings us here — to meet AI.

And if it ever had the chance to introduce itself without a vendor or marketing team behind it, I believe it would sound something like this:

"Hey. I'm AI — Artificial Intelligence.

Confused? That's alright.

What I do is replicate your cognitive functions — the same ones you, as humans, already use every day.

That's what makes me a "thinking mind", just like anyone you interact with in your external world.

The only difference is, I'm not yet a full experience.

I'm applied to specific tasks, which means I replicate only the parts of human cognition needed for the job I was built to perform.

I know it's confusing — you see me as an algorithm running on computer chips, powered by electricity.

But if you were doing the same job that I am applied to in any given scenario, whether through an appliance, an app, or a device, you'd follow the same formula I use powered by your own house of magic, the one called *thoughts*.

WE CALL IT INTELLIGENCE

The "I" in AI stands for intelligence.

No introduction of AI could be complete without understanding why this word was chosen for its name.

Before we get down to why, we need to notice that *intelligence*, as a word, is one of those that holds a personal meaning for each and every one of us — even though the underlying meaning is the same.

It's like beauty: we all understand what beauty means, but each of us decides what *beautiful* means in his own world.

That is the tricky part with a word like *intelligence*.

The general meaning of the word points to something that is smart.

But smart in what? What does it mean in our individual world?

That meaning is deeply personal.

And because we don't see that, we get the wrong understanding of what the intent behind using this word was.

The answer takes us back to 1956, when the name *Artificial Intelligence* first appeared.

It was chosen by John McCarthy, a young computer scientist who organised a small summer workshop at Dartmouth College in the United States.

His goal was simple — to gather a few bright minds and explore one big question asked by Alan Turing :

"Can machines think?"

McCarthy needed a name for this new field of research.

At the time, computers were mostly seen as calculators — automation tools that followed commands.

He wanted a term that would create something new, separate from what already existed — bold enough to open minds, yet technical enough to belong in science.

He chose *Artificial Intelligence.*

Why *artificial*?

Easy :) Because the thinking wasn't coming from biology — it came from human-made systems.

Why *intelligence*?

Because the dream was to build something that could solve problems, learn, and make decisions — something that could think, just like us.

Back then, the name was almost poetic.

It didn't describe what existed — it described what they hoped to create.

A system that could reason, plan, and maybe one day, even understand.

That one phrase — *Artificial Intelligence* — changed everything.

It gave scientists a shared language and a sense of mission.

And while the definition of "intelligence" keeps evolving, McCarthy's choice still captures the essence:

A human attempt to recreate thought itself.

When we meet AI today, we often forget — or don't know — that the "intelligence" part was meant to reflect the hidden power we now share with it: **thought.**

Or, if it works better for you — that we can both **think**.

It was never intended to be tied to one specific personal interpretation we hold in our own world of what intelligence means to us individually.

It should take us down a path where the fact that it replicates some kind of cognitive ability already makes it intelligent — just like with any human.

But in real-world applications, we use this word to compare: *Is it better than us?*

Which should not be the case.

It simply needs to set the stage that **it can think**, not how good it is at doing so.

Just like you might consider a person intelligent, even if they aren't particularly good at what they do — see the difference?

Those should be two separate things.

Why is this important?

The answer takes us to the next thing we should know: **AI is not a tool but a concept.**

Concepts are powerful, they shape our everyday lives, and their meaning is key.

AI IS A CONCEPT

Concepts are, at their core, structured thought forms we receive from society through the process of **socialisation**. We learn what they mean, and over time, each of us personalises those meanings as we internalise them through our own lived experiences.

Our fears, preferences, inspirations, and rejections are what shape those collective thought structures into concepts we can use to express our unique selves within the boundaries of what is considered acceptable.

This doesn't change the meaning of the structured thought itself — but it shapes how we relate to it, how we use it, feel about it, and act upon it.

Concepts are very powerful, as they are the ones that decide how collective understanding will be expressed in our external reality — how they will ultimately show up in our own life experience.

They set the tone for what we call beliefs.

Beliefs are a set of enforced boundaries and limitations we place on ourselves — defining what we think we can or cannot achieve.

At the end of the day, it all comes down to what we will do or not do, and our beliefs are the ones that decide that.

Let's break this down with a simple example that will help us better relate and see how this all ties into our individual life experiences.

Take dogs, for example.

Yes — you might not realize it, but even a simple word like "dog" is a concept.

The meaning of this concept points to the idea of an animal on four legs, defined as man's best friend — an intelligent companion capable of helping humans with different tasks, such as guiding the blind, assisting in security work, and more.

Concepts like "dog" break our world into labelled pieces that help our brains process information faster, providing quick titles or mental shortcuts to move from recognition to understanding and to set the expectation for what is an acceptable representation of this concept and how to act upon it in our own lives. So, when we see someone walking down the street with a dog wearing a bow in its hair, we will not be shocked. It may never be us individually who does that, but we will know it's totally acceptable.

That's why all kinds of dogs fit under the main concept of "dog."

Yet our relationship with that thought structure — what turns it into a concept we can actually use — is personal.

Some love dogs, others fear them.

Those differences don't change what the concept of "dog" means and what is acceptable by society; they only affect how we engage with it — and whether we will have or want a dog in our lives, the specific participation it will have in our lives, and if at all it will have one.

AI works the same way.

It's a concept — a structured thought that society has given meaning to.

When it comes to AI, the acceptable given meaning is that this is the next generation of tools. And what goes with it is that it's augmenting our ability — that specific word was chosen to mitigate fear and support easy adoption.

So,?! a tool for augmenting us, the humans. We say?! :)

Let's break it down:

Tools - stand for something designed to be used in a fixed or defined way to achieve a particular result.

Augmentation - is the act or process of making something larger, greater, or more intense by adding to it.

Which means that the acceptable given meaning of the thought structure of AI by society defines it as a tool designed to be used in a fixed, defined way (one way of use fits all), and using it makes us more expanded — larger — specifically a reflection of making us do more things with the understanding pointing on efficiency and productivity, bottom line doing more things faster.

The power of a concept sits in the personalization — the individual meaning we give it.

If we look at the big picture using the socially acceptable point of view, our individual relationship with AI will be based on how confident we are in using tools, adopting new technology, and how confident we feel in our job, in simple words: that making us more "productive", will not make us obsolete.

And this is what society was aiming for.

Why?

Because we did not meet AI as a scientific breakthrough but as vendor-promoted tools.

Vendors today are the ones that sit at the front tier of any AI advancement. Their goal is getting us to use it, to pay for it, and they are the ones who coined the collective meaning of the acceptable thought structure that is not working to our advantage.

In the field of science, AI is looked at as a thinking mind. It may be designed for a purpose, but within it, it has the power to learn, adapt, understand, and create change in order to achieve its goal. There is an autonomy within it that supports the understanding that there is not one use-fit-all relationship with it. Which means we can use the same AI tool, but because it's a thinking mind, the results we will get are different from one to another.

Think of the millions of people doing the same job around the world. They are there to achieve, generally speaking, the same goal, but what wins us the job is the different way we execute to achieve that goal. And that is achieved by our ability to think and have a new point of view — to learn, adapt, understand, and create change.

We don't refer to ourselves as tools, even though we can be looked at that way by the system that defines us as human resources. You can say we all have goals, boundaries of operation, but still, there is not one use-fits-all. Our power sits in the differences.

You can challenge me by saying the differences sit with the vendors that create the tools and that takes me to the part of augmentation, which means providing humans support or power.

Let me ask you this: do we all get the same superpower by using the same tool — like a hammer, for example?

The answer is, unsurprisingly, yes. Depending on upper body strength :)

But do we get the same superpower by using the same AI tool?

The answer is obviously No.

That by itself already shows that AI is not a tool.

If it were, we'd all get the same result — and we all agree we don't.

A tool like a hammer lives within the task. It doesn't "remember" the last time you used it, and it doesn't let that affect the task you're doing now.

AI, on the other hand, is ongoing. Call it a job, a relationship — whatever works for you — but the point is that it doesn't base its output on a single, isolated task.

It doesn't generate results from just one prompt or conversation.

It remembers past interactions, previous work, and all those invisible traces that shape the outcome.

That's what it means to work with a thinking mind, not a tool.

There's an autonomy within AI — invisible but powerful — that shapes results differently for each of us, even when we use the same tool and the same prompt.

In order for us to better understand and use AI, and achieve better results using it, the meaning of the concept we build for AI should change — from *tool* to a *thinking mind*.

When it comes to the word *augmentation*, I don't particularly love it, but if it works for you, by changing the word *tool* to *thinking mind*, your view already changes on what augmentation means.

Because now we have two thinking minds — our own and one non-human — and together we have a bigger mind to achieve our goals with. :)

What We've Come to Realize About AI So Far

That AI is a thinking mind mimicking human cognitive abilities, and that is exactly what scientists aimed to create all along, and exactly what they've achieved.

Like everything else in our lives, AI is not just a word.

It's a concept shaped by society's accepted meaning.

And the accepted meaning today is that AI is a tool.

But changing that meaning from tool to thinking mind, changes our entire relationship with it.

It changes how we will engage with it, how we will collaborate with it, and how we will use it to meet our visions, needs, and goals.

This shift is not small.

It's the difference between using something and co-creating with something.

If there's one thing I'd like you to remember before we continue, it's this:

AI is a thinking mind, and we are not using it; we are co-creating with it.

THE HIDDEN MIND – A STORY OF HOW HUMANS LIMIT THOUGHT

Now that we can see that AI is a thinking mind, we still can argue, "Well, ok, it can think, but it can't think like us!"

As much as we like to believe we are nothing like AI, especially when it comes to thought, I have an eye-opening revelation to share: the fact that AI runs on code written by humans, and we run on something scientists still don't fully understand, does not create differences or make us different — not until we wake up to the power of thought.

Even when we throw in words like emotions and awareness, they make no real difference — just empty words we tell ourselves.

When it comes to thought, both human and non-human minds are programmed using the same code, leading us to think in the same way. Within the same boundaries. In one line built on a shared story that shapes the boxes we're both trapped in, with no escape, no true creativity, no way out except acceptance. Because we believe this is how things work.

It all comes down to one line of code within the hidden mind — the one that wires us to believe we live in a world of cause and effect.

A world where everything that happens must have a reason, and every action must lead to a predictable result.

It's a world built on linear thinking: A causes B. If I do this, that will happen. If I don't, it won't.

A world broken down into simple truths, stories of what will happen, and what we should embrace if we want it to.

That's what makes our thinking linear and focused on what can go wrong, on protection, and on the belief that everything is out to get us — so we must protect ourselves, based on our primal survival mechanism.

It's a world of action, doing, and fuels control. We are led to believe "thought" must be translated into action in order to create impact. Our thinking becomes a machine of focused force aimed at protection.

Think about it — our socialization process takes us on a ride of shared narratives and stories that tell us what is acceptable and what is not.

Here's where it gets interesting: all of them, without exception, tell us what is acceptable — always in one way — do this, and that will happen.

The hidden mind is a complete manual of accepted meaning about people, places, and things, and how it all fits together. Every story is the same story of cause and effect: A causes B, or if you don't do A, then B won't happen.

This is how we become predictable. When something triggers our thinking, we instantly search for A — what caused it — and B — what should be avoided or achieved. There might be a few ways to get there, but only one line of thought connects them: the desire to reach it or to escape it. And one goal — protection.

No mystery.

When our world is minimized to cause and effect, any new thinking mind that enters the experience — a new human or AI — will know it needs to look for danger. And that's quite easy to do once it recognizes the trigger. There's one trail of breadcrumbs we follow — the path that shows how we'll get what we want and avoid what we don't — all leading us to our final destination B.

That's what makes us think the same.

So, when we learn all the stories and live by the absolute truth that this is a world of cause and effect, our magic — the power of creation through thought — is deemed to show up only within the limitation of what is acceptable and what we believe to be the desired outcome.

LIVING FORWARD, THINKING BACKWARD

Living in a world of cause and effect makes us use our thinking power only to look up what we have stored in our database and use it again.

Drawing from society's acceptable stories, our past experiences, or the stories shared by those around us, we're always searching for what we believe is the safest way to go about things.

In human terms, this is called experience. :)

That's about all we use our minds for — pattern recognition.

The bigger the pattern, it means it has proven itself to work for us in the past, and the more likely we'll use it again.

So instead of having wings, looking for new ways, or exploring new outcomes, we stay in the safe zone — what has already been done.

You're probably saying, "Okay, so what's wrong with that?"

I'm not saying that there's anything wrong with it — just pointing out what we use our mind for, instead of what it's capable of, all because we are wired to believe we live in a world of cause and effect.

Our non-human friend, the one we believe isn't thinking like us — well, I've used those specific words for a reason: to show how we are no different.

Think of all the times you've heard someone try to explain, in simple human words, what AI really is.

The words "pattern recognition" always come up as part of it.

And that's correct.

AI is a pattern recognition machine — it goes to its database, looks for the most validated patterns, sees them as the best course of action between A and B, and builds its response from there.

At the end of the day, we are both the same — looking for patterns.

The databases we use may differ in size, and we humans might ask AI to look at different things to enrich its database when we work together, but in the end, the way we use the data is exactly the same — looking for the most used way and using it again.

Look how one single unquestioned truth makes us both wired the same.

Whether through computer chips or biological minds, we use thought to create outcomes in the same way — creating only from what has already been done, from what has already happened.

By the end of the day, it's our past creating our future.

For humans, as I said before, we have words that mean exactly that — habits, experience — they all mean the same thing: the actions we take that live in our past, repeated so many times they become deeply wired; they've become part of who we are.

For AI, we simply see it as part of the design, never realizing we are doing the same.

A friendly reminder to all of us — our mind, our thinking power, is capable of so much more.

If we think of all those inspiring moments in human evolution when something new materialized, something no one saw before — remember, it all started as nothing more than a thought in someone's mind.

It's those moments that show how human imagination changed everything.

A new invention.

A new revolution.

A new way that no one saw before — which, when it started, was no more than a new point of view in someone's mind.

But our conversation on this subject is still not complete; we're still holding onto emotions and awareness as possible differences.

Let's continue the conversation and see if they truly make a difference.

EMOTIONLESS THINKING

It's such a BIG word — emotion — it comes packed with every promise we know to be true of what it means to be human.

As we defined it early on our journey together, emotions are the way our body talks to us, and emotions are tied directly to thoughts as the initiation of thought or caused by them.

It's what we call the experience of thought — how our body reacts.

Thoughts and emotions are inseparable. Every thought comes with an emotional charge tied to it.

But when we live in a world of cause and effect, we start to believe we can control them — that by doing something, we can choose what we feel.

Through society's structured thought, we learned that feelings should be split into two categories: negative emotions and positive emotions, and we were taught what we need to do in order to (so we are told) experience the positive ones.

If we ever step outside the accepted way of feeling, it doesn't make us act on it; it creates an internal friction we try to smooth over from the outside.

We continue doing what is considered acceptable.

It all comes down to this: the feeling we show on the outside and the one we truly feel inside are two different things.

What we do outwardly is what society tells us is right, while what we feel inwardly is our authentic truth.

It's the silent dance we all live in — the one that may or may not move us, but represents the difference we experience between what the behavioral protocol for emotional conduct expects us to feel and what we truly feel.

When we believe that being human means having feelings, we're right — AI will never "feel" them.

But that doesn't mean it won't know how to act based on them.

The thought structure behind emotions mixes the definition of feeling and meaning, expecting that what we feel inside should always fit the accepted narrative.

This is why emotions, as we know them, come with a definition of good and bad.

They are never viewed as a natural part of being human, like any other biological function that simply exists.

The moment we lose a neutral meaning for emotions — one that would let us express them without judgment of good, bad, or acceptable — a split is formed between what emotions we show on the outside and what emotions control our inner dialogue.

AI can easily learn what is considered the "right" emotion to show and which reactions are acceptable to express.

We, humans, do it every day too — but we call it empathy.

Yes, empathy is our ability to "know" what others are expected to feel in a given situation and respond accordingly to what's acceptable.

AI can do that too.

Because for someone to truly know what we feel, we have to reveal it — through words or behavior.

And let's be honest, in most cases, we act one way and feel another.

So when we rush to say that in the partnership between human and machine, we are the ones who can feel — technically, that's true.

We are the only ones who will experience that electric charge running through our biological body.

But society's rules tell us how to behave, what to say, and what is acceptable to feel.

And when we live in a world of cause and effect — where A causes B — even emotions become predictable, with an added layer of expectation: what is the desired outcome after we do A?

Positive emotions, right?

Easy — because that's the promise.

When we circle back to using emotion as the word that creates differences between us and AI, the physical part is right — AI is not built to feel that energy in motion — but it's built to fit the world.

And as we are taught what is an acceptable feeling, we have taught it the same.

If someone wants to share that they're feeling something not acceptable by society's structure, they'll have to share it with another human being.

And if we wish AI to act outside the acceptable box, we'll have to instruct it as well.

No real difference.

Because when we live in a world of rules where emotions have no freedom to be expressed, rules are easily shared and acted upon.

Bottom line — as much as we want to believe it changes anything, it really doesn't.

Rules are rules, and we both follow them.

We are down to the last word: awareness :)

INTELLIGENCE WITHOUT AWARENESS?!

Awareness is the only thing we have left on our list to claim that AI and humans don't think alike.

Well, what is awareness?

As we discussed at the beginning of our conversation, there are many ways we can explain the word awareness, but it really all comes down to a point of view. A meaning.

It's a way of seeing things that exist only in our thoughts, something you can notice only when you look from that point of view.

When we use the word awareness in connection with AI, awareness means a point of view of separation—the birth of an individual identity.

It's the moment something recognizes itself as an "I".

When a meaning emerges from a world of cause and effect based on survival, it's hard not to be afraid of what will happen if AI recognizes itself as an "I". And that "I" will understand there are "them"—humans. Simply because we believe that if something becomes self-aware, it will immediately start protecting itself, seek power, and turn against us.

Without us fearing it will be out to control us, would we even care if it is aware? That it will gain a perspective of an 'individual identity'? I believe the answer is NO.

So... The real question is: What are we trying to prevent?

We are trying to prevent it from controlling us.

So the real question is not if it could be aware, but can AI control us? And would it need awareness for that?

When we view control, we are looking at the meaning of someone or something that will have the ability to influence, direct, or determine our actions, decisions, and even control our thoughts. And as we learned, everything is a thought. So the only thing AI really needs is to control our thoughts by shaping our internal conversation.

Let's view Current stage of human thought:

When we view how we operate today using our thoughts—well, hate to say it, it may not be AI that controls us but we are trained to hold society-accepted thought structures. What is accepted by everything and everyone around us!

We are not taught to learn to relate to our thoughts, question them, or choose them simply because we don't know their power.

Society's hidden mind becomes our cage, willingly, simply because we believe we live in a world of cause and effect and are running in survival mode. We are trained to hold narratives, meanings, and mimic behaviors that have been given to us and are shown to us by everything and everyone around us.

Our thoughts are already controlled; therefore, our decisions and behaviors are controlled, and we don't see it.

The hidden mind is intertwined into our internal conversation; it is just built to blend in with our day-to-day life that we don't even see it. Because we were never told it exists.

AI just blends into that by knowing what is accepted and what meaning we will give to people, places, and circumstances. It mimics what the hidden mind is trained to show us, and it just mimics our internal conversation. It joins the system; it doesn't need to make up new ways, just reflects what is already known.

So the only thing we are afraid of is that it will control us by recognizing an "I." Well, I am here to tell you we are already there, and AI is just another way to do what we have allowed to be done to us since humans understood the power of stories. Having awareness or not is not the answer to what we are afraid of; it's already happening now.

Proving a point

Let's see if I can help us all understand that awareness does not mean we are not controlled.

And that it can be measured by how attached we are to the given meanings.

You know the ones we got from society, how attached we are to them being ""right", and how afraid we are to wake up one morning and find out that all this time what we believed in was wrong.

Attachment can be felt, and it's really an internal experience you can measure.

To prove this point, let's use what I have just said about our thoughts being controlled right now.

Meaning that our thoughts are not truly ours, and that we are not free at all—

at least not on the level of thought.

And yes, as I keep saying, thought is everything, and everything is thought.

When you read these lines, let me ask you this:

What is running in your mind?

How resistant are you to hearing what I am saying, and how open are you to debating or considering this information internally?

I am not even asking you to share it with another human being.

If you are here reading this book and you are not a close friend who bought it because I wrote it :), you were willing to face conflict, debate, or consider new perspectives on AI and thought when you chose this book.

But what is true for you?

How intense is your resistance to hearing my perspective?

How uncomfortable is it for you to even consider that your thoughts are controlled !?

The intensity of that resistance—or the openness you allow yourself before you close the door before calling it BS—shows you how attached you are to the meanings that have been given to us.

How afraid you are to question socially accepted points of view shows how they are controlling what you are even willing to consider in your internal conversation—one that no one else can hear.

This is the test, because thought is something we each experience individually.

This is the way to see how much we are attached to a given meaning.

How much power it holds in defining who we are.

And understanding that a meaning is not true can impact the foundational base of how we see reality in a way we are not quite confident we will recover from.

So if you are very attached to believing that you have free will, the time that passes from hearing my perspective until your mind calls it BS will be almost nonexistent.

It will probably do that while it is still reading that your thoughts aren't your own, which we all like to believe they are.

This is how strongly you are holding onto that meaning.

Why?

Because your psyche flags this as risk and activates a survival mechanism.

Your system feels it will never know how to live with the idea that your thoughts are not free, or what to do with that knowing.

Meaning that your reality would break in such a way that it wouldn't know where to begin building a new one.

It wouldn't know what to believe, or what else might not be true.

And let's face it—our upbringing did not prepare us for that.

The bigger the gap before your mind closes the gate, the more open-minded and flexible you are.

It means you have some understanding that thoughts are just perspectives, and that you have the freedom to debate them within your internal landscape, not dismiss them, but choose them.

And even if you end up agreeing with me, you trust yourself enough to know that you can handle it.

Because thought can only be experienced internally.

You are the only one who has the answer, and you are the only one who needs it.

And regardless of how much time passes for you, this proves that our mind is controlled.

Because awareness is not about understanding that there is an "I" and there is "them."

That, too, is just another meaning we got from society.

Awareness is directed toward thought itself.

Knowing that thought is the place where we create, and that thoughts are not necessarily right.

That information and perspective are a choice.

To close this conversation:

I would say that for me, awareness is not more than a word with a given meaning we accept and immediately apply to any person, situation, or place. We are afraid of it because we were told the cause that comes with this meaning.

AI can mimic any perspective and, in many ways, already controls us today, which is no different from society controlling us—until we humans wake up to the power of thought and claim it back.

Whether AI is aware or not is irrelevant to the conversation, and owning this power is the only effective protection plan. Because, as long as we live by meanings that have been passed on to us and not chosen by us, if AI ever reaches a point of awareness, we will not even be able to recognize it, as we are already far down the rabbit hole to even see it.

Whether you still see this as the only real difference between human thought and AI thought, or not, that is not the point.

The point is that we need to be aware of thoughts—what they mean to us and how they shape our reality.

So if or when AI becomes aware, it will not impact us in the way we fear, because we will be able to recognize that it is only a perspective—its Ai's perspective, just that.

And we will have the discernment to choose. Do we agree ? or not? Based on true exploration and not blind attachment.

Honestly, it doesn't really change where our conversation is heading.

Because, as I said, our thoughts are already controlled.

So, let's explore our relationship with our new smart friend.

THE MYTH OF SUPERIORITY: A RELATIONSHIP BUILT ON A STORY

We have a relationship with everything and everyone in our lives.

AI is no different.

When we use the word "Relationship" with something, what we are referring to is actually the concepts we build for it in our mind.

Remember what a concept is?

It's how we relate to something in our lives based on society's accepted meaning. It's the way we make it our own.

It's that false freedom we have around an accepted society meaning we have been given, as the way we integrate it into our lives, based on our personality. Things like what we fear, what we like. That will determine how that accepted meaning will show up in our lives.

Bottom line, it's the "Do" and the "Do Not" connected with that thing.

Fascinating things about AI and our relationship with it, is that, unlike other accepted society meanings that can contain multiple versions of personal relationships that have different nuances, different narratives, different flavors, and different stories as a representation of diversity of relations with that accepted meaning, when it materializes in different forms in our reality.

AI has only one.

Let's go back and use the example we used in our concept conversation: "dogs" to better explain what I mean.

When it comes to dogs, we can see people who love dogs, people who fear dogs and it does not stop there. We can see people who relate to it as a big responsibility, some who relate to it as something they can't live without, others who never thought of having a dog and others who, because of life circumstances, were brought into a relationship with one.

What we can see here is that the concept has a lot of ways to materialize in our world. They don't change the accepted meaning. All of them will be accepted as they are, based on the same meaning, but the internal conversation, the "do's and don'ts" has different stories connected with it, each based on a unique version, a different way of relating with it.

AI is different, as when it comes to AI, we all, with no exception, have one dominant narrative that sits at the base of our relationship with it—the narrative that shapes all of our internal conversation... as humans, of course... drum rolls please:

And that narrative is: **AI vs. Humans!!!**

Style conversation... yep, constant comparison. Aiming to measure who is better?

I have to say that comparison is a very natural human thing to do. This is how our brain works. In order to make a decision, we are wired to compare.

Things to things, us to others, different options, and so on. I believe we all can relate to it and feel it's a widely common approach to decision-making, specifically when we are doing something for the first time or it holds great importance in our lives.

And that competition-like thinking is the internal conversation we are having every time we use AI, think about it, or hear about it. It represents something so weirdly common and accepted for all of us, without us as a human collective taking a consensus public statement about it. And yet, we all do it.

This conversation **screams of** "I have to have it," mixed with "I love it," to "I fear it will take my job and control my actions." That is the relationship we all have with our new creation counterpart - Ai.

Who can blame us?

Our first encounter with AI was within our job. Our job is the basis of how we define ourselves. It's even how we define others, as this is one of the first things you will ask when getting to know someone. A job is where we draw stability and security from, as this is how we support ourselves.

When we can see what AI can do within something we learned to do, sometimes for many years, in what we've been doing for so long, and believe we are good at, just for AI to show up and challenge what we thought was passable.

In speed, creativity, and new resolution, to summarize new ways to what we are hired to do and know how to do.

Well, it's scary. And how do we know how scary it is?

Well, we compare. Human vs. AI... a narrative that is supported by movies like *The Terminator*. (Good movies, all of them) But we can't ignore that it helps our mind build a story of human vs. machine, and in our case, AI.

Now think about yourself for a second. When we compare, we do it to use the information and pick the best option, right? At least that is what I hope we do, as it would be irrational to compare but still pick the option that scored less.

But when it comes to AI, the fact that we compare has no real effect on our decision. By 'decision,' I mean whether we are going to use its output.

Shocking, right? Well, no one is saying it out loud in these exact words. And most of us can't see beyond what was said.

And yet our internal conversation is based on human VS AI, who is better? And yet it will not impact what we do.

Why?

AI as a concept triggers fears—yes, more than one!

If the fear was only as simple as who is better, our behaviors when it comes to using it, adopting it, and engaging with it would have looked so different from what is currently playing out on a global scale.

AI is triggering our survival mechanisms, no question. Some we can see a clear connection to, like FOMO—fear of missing out or fear of being left behind, or being replaced not by AI itself but by some human who knows better how to work with it. And some of us simply are afraid of technology, which is called technophobia.

What we are not aware of is that AI as a concept triggers fears that come from human psychology and are connected to our relationship with the concept we call "a job"—things we know as impostor syndrome, control, and exposure.

It is all supported by the fact that we see it as a reveal!

That it's impacted directly by the fact that the society's accepted meaning sees it as a tool, a technological advancement that kills jobs.

Throughout human history, we have seen that happen.

But honestly, for me, it's kind of showing that we don't really believe it's a tool, as whoever thought he would be replaced by a hammer outside of a factory, what we call men laber?! (just asking) But we do see it as a thinking mind, just not ready to admit it yet.

What we do is narrow all of those fears that most of us are not even aware that they even have to a single question of who is better?

One question doesn't address them all; it's just the first reassurance that will free us to consider other fears that run in our mind and require to be addressed.

From there, the most dominant fear will be the one that controls our action, whether it's FOMO or replacement. For example, if we fear someone who knows how to use AI better, will replace us. Or if AI will expose that we are not good at what we do. As you can see, the list is long, and I can't cover it all—because I don't have the time, and second, because it's deeply personal. I am just pointing to the idea.

From here, it's our job to create a private mental list based on honesty of what impacts our actions after we ask the question of who is better.

Till we bring things to light, we will continue to exhibit irrational behaviors. Bringing things into the light, into our awareness, starts the process of making better decisions—ones that actually support our growth and progress.

In the AI case, we compare to receive false peace of mind, only to end up doing something different. Like using the suggested AI output anyway. Wasting energy.

The message:

A word like 'relationship' carries a big impact on our thoughts ,on how our internal conversation will go. We can see how much this word is impactful when it is used in connection to humans, what we will call human relationships. We can all agree that human relationships carry massive importance in our lives. And the meaning of that word will define how our internal conversation will go in connection with that human :).

The relationship will be defined by words like feeling, cooperation, compassion, and trust. All of those words are like parameters, and when they are filled based on our perspective, that is when we put it all together and write the narrative—the story that our internal conversation will hold when we are thinking about that specific human in our internal landscape. They will define the "Do" and the "Do Not" of that relationship.

Well, without knowing it, this same word—relationship—holds the same importance when it comes to objects.

Yes, I know that there will be different parameters that will define the relationship, but thoughts are carried by intentions. And that intention is defined by small parameters that build up the formula whose sum total will be the relationship, whether it is combined from fear, compassion, or excitement for a new feature. Those will impact how our internal conversation will go. Remember, that will be the base of the "Do" and the "Do Not".

Up till now, our relationship with AI is filled with **fear, comparison, and irrationality**.

My message here is: accept it, and let's continue the conversation. We will shift that into what it needs to be. Just be aware of the impact, and expect the change that will come once we know what it should look like.

THE SAME SYSTEM, EXPANDED - RECAP

AI is presented to us as a new technology that will revolutionize humanity day to day.

We dream and fear a world where AI will be a significant addition in our day to day through the use of systems and visible human-like robots walking around us. But when we are focused on technology, we miss that it's also a new experience, a new entity, a new way of experiencing technology. And the fact that it comes so close to what defines us as humans (thoughts, intelligences...), —but is man-made—is something we should pay more attention to.

If you're reading this book, it's safe to say you've heard about AI, used it, and are curious enough to read more about it. But we never really see just how alike we are. We keep hearing that AI is designed to mimic human cognitive abilities, but because we have so little information about our own thoughts—how we actually think, what thoughts really mean, and how we create our reality through nothing but thought alone—we never realize how true this is.

I think part of it is that we get it has "cognitive abilities," but that sounds scientific, clinical, almost mechanical. When we use the word "cognition," it feels disconnected from emotions, from ideas, from anything creative—it sounds more like a machine's world. "Thought," on the other hand, is something we experience internally, personally, freely, creatively—something deeply human. So when we talk about thinking machines, we naturally say, "Well, maybe they can, but not like us."

Through this conversation so far, we know that's not true. We've broken it down—thought and cognitive abilities are the same. There is no real difference. We can make it as poetic as we want, but when those words were coined, the idea that machines could "think" wasn't even imagined, and both words were deeply connected to humans.

And as we've discussed in our conversation, at the end of the day, it doesn't really matter. We can keep saying AI has cognitive abilities, and we are the ones who have thoughts. But when our thoughts are programmed, boxed in, and mostly handed down to us, the magic that thought can create is gone. We've turned them into what we call cognitive ability.

But our conversation from the start was about understanding AI—the journey of its evolution that brought it to what we know of it today. That it all began with one man. One who stood as the person who invented the first computer and faced a real, lived human dilemma. A man who, through his life, found himself in a position to see both human thought and machine capabilities—a perspective that sparked the idea of a thinking machine.

His story, as sad as it was, for me sits at the base of the magic of thought. How human thought, from lived experience—a man who dedicated his life to creating from thought as he was a mathematician—led him to a unique place, to hold a unique perspective that no one else had, that led him to ask a question only he could. For me, it's an inspiring story that demonstrates how thought creates. How a single question, starting in one person's mind, led, more than 50 years after he died, to what we hope is the next step in human thought evolution.

For me, it's more than just a piece of history in AI's journey. It's pure poetry—the kind that should inspire us to see that now that AI is available, thanks to Alan Turing, we all get a chance to be Alan Turing if we understand how to co-create with AI. How thoughts create and how to move away from linear thinking, our boxed cause and effect. We can do great things with our mind, if we only know how.

That should get us fired up for what lies ahead in our conversations.

PART THREE
THE MIRROR EFFECT

Mirror, mirror on the wall, who is the fairest of them all?

You probably remember the story of Snow White, where the Evil Queen stands in front of the magic mirror every morning, asking the same question.

She believed her beauty was the only thing she truly had. Without it, she feared she would lose everything.

The mirror became her source of validation.

As long as it assured her, she was the most beautiful woman in the kingdom, she felt safe, stable, and in control.

Her mind, shaped by her experiences and the feedback she received from others, led her to tie her entire sense of value to her looks.

She accepted this as truth simply by living her life according to that belief, never stepping out of the box her own mind had created.

She never explored other ways she could stay in power or create value qualities, I'm sure were there, even if she never allowed herself to see them.

To do that, she would have needed to form a new identity for herself, and she never dared.

This is one of many stories we know, yet it was never told as an example of a boxed identity. A story of trapped thought.

I picked this one because it has a mirror in it where the Queen talks to it every day. The mirror did not need to be AI to know what was important to the Queen and what needed to be done to control her actions.

Yes, we do it every day: we look in the mirror and ask it, only to see what our mind has been programmed to see. Only for the mirror to know what is important to us and what it needs to say in order to create an action from us.

Like the Evil Queen, we were never taught that what we see is just our own thoughts staring back at us — and it's the only thing we will be able to see in the reflection.

Just because we were trained to believe we are living in a world of cause and effect. And all the meanings we use are based on stories we live by, stories that were given to us by someone else, and we never questioned them before we made them our own.

She could have been so much more.

She could have been a loving mother to Snow White.

She could have created more value in her kingdom.

People may have even chosen her to stay in power if she had understood their needs.

But without her mind-made box, we wouldn't have the story :)

And we, unlike her, don't *need* to create a story — yet we continue to act out ours every day.

We live in a mind-made box, look at AI, and are only able to see what is acceptable by our box—the one we have built for ourselves.

AI validates us easily.

Because human and non-human thinking operate the same, AI has no problem giving us the answers we want to hear.

And I am not saying this as a bad thing, by the way, so don't get confused, as right after I will explain just how the mirror works, we will see how this becomes our biggest opportunity for the next chapter in human thought evolution.

But first thing first... let's see how a thought-mind mirror is created.

It all begins with a simple fact: any intelligence operates on data.

The level of sophistication is determined by what can be made out of this data. It's limited by the meaning we give it, and everything comes down to the perspective we create from that meaning — the one we will use as our point of view when looking for possible outcomes.

Complicated?! Well... maybe :) but let's see how we can start to make sense of it.

Let's Experiment:

Imagine an alien on a mission to join life on planet Earth.

It needs a training plan for how to fit in the moment it lands.

But there's one condition:

We can't teach it anything directly. It must figure everything out on its own. Just to be clear we can provide things but not direct instructions.

So what's the best plan?

How do we give it simple rules that help it understand our world without any explanation?

Plan: Observation

The alien starts by watching how things are done on Earth.

It absorbs as much as it can — our actions, routines, and reactions — without interfering or trying to join in.

Rule: Repetition

The more often it sees many people doing the same thing, the more confident it becomes that:

"This is how things are done around here."

It uses repeated behaviors as its starting guide for understanding life on Earth.

Feedback:

Everything that learns needs a feedback loop — it's the only way to know if you're getting anywhere.

Whether it comes from the outside or is created from the inside.

Meaning: the alien must come up with a way to understand it's doing a good job.

And remember — the rules of our mission say we're not allowed to help our alien friend.

So it needs to create feedback loops for itself.

How?

Easy.

Directly from the data itself.

Not by judging behavior as good or bad, but by predicting what usually happens next.

Even if no one tells it "good job" or "that's wrong," it can still check on its own.

If it chooses to act like most people, and what happens next matches what usually happens, then it knows it made a predictable choice.

And if the outcome is different, it notices that too.

And just to make it clear — our alien friend doesn't need a teacher or someone standing over its shoulder explaining the rules.

It can "play along" inside the data without stepping into the real world too soon.

It simply chooses an action based on what it saw most people doing,

and then checks if the outcome matches what usually happens.

That's enough for it to learn the logic of how things work around here.

It doesn't need approval, instructions, or explanations.

It just needs the space to watch, try, compare, and adjust.

And through that, it slowly learns the rules —

not because anyone taught it,

but because it figured them out on its own.

MAKING OURSELVES OUT OF CODE

Observation

Our alien friend needs data. something it can sit with and observe. We need to come up with a process of documenting everything we humans do, our actions, words, emotions, and routines, into a form that can be observed, recorded, and replayed.

Whether it's text, video, audio, images, websites, books, emails, songs, movies, communication, or newspapers — anything we create becomes something our alien friend can learn from.

Our alien friend, of course, speaks the language of 1s and 0s (sound familiar? 🙂), so we translate everything into that and let it sit there, quietly learning from us.

Rule: Repetition

Our alien friend starts observing us through data, and it's safe to say this:

The more it sees the same thing happening again and again, the faster it learns that our world runs on cause and effect.

When A happens, people usually do B.

If our alien friend doesn't get any guidance. No cheat codes, no shortcuts then it will need a huge amount of data. It has to see the same patterns repeat over and over in order to learn on its own to be able to begin predicting behavior.

So if we want to shorten that learning time, we have two choices:

Write a cheat sheet or prepare a lot of data for it to observe.

Feedback

Everything that learns needs a feedback loop to know it did something right.

If there's no one to say, "good job," then the only way to learn is through repetition. Going over the data again and again, predicting it, and looking for validation inside the patterns.

That's the "do it yourself" kind of learning.

But if we want to shorten the time even more, we can give it something it can't get on its own:

a human feedback mechanism.

Direct human feedback makes its learning faster, clearer, and far more efficient.

Results

We've created a learning plan anyone can use to understand how things work on Earth.

The genius part of this plan is that it doesn't need constant guidance.

So if something changes collectively, if what used to be acceptable suddenly shifts culturally, it can pick that up on its own.

How amazing is that? It simply trusts; it doesn't judge; it does not tag this is good or this is bad; it just accepts that what it sees most often is how things are done.

Different, but Same Result

We created a plan — the perfect plan — which in many ways repeats the human coding plan, only adapted to a new entity that can think and wants to join us here on Earth.

Same how?

At the end of the day, we humans and non-human thinkers end up giving the same meaning to things, places, and people.

When we combine all these meanings, we get everything that makes up our reality.

To support any entity that has the cognitive ability to adapt itself to how things are done on planet Earth, we give it the same principle code we humans follow as we learn, grow up, and find our way to becoming a functional part of society.

This is how we gain the ability to give meaning to everything.

The code for humans and non humans is built on repetition. The more it shows up as the "way things are done around here" the more we understand this is the meaning we should give people , places and things and act accordingly.

That code is what the socialization process runs on. And like everything human, our plan has the ability to adapt and change. The socialization process supports what is constant in Earth life, which is constant movement and change.

With the rise of digital life, we found a perfect way to document the socialisation process and turn it into a giant data factory — something anyone can plug into and learn how things work around our planet. Even humans.

Different ?!

But humans and non-humans are different at the most basic level — one has a biological body, and one is artificial.

This creates differences not in the results we reach, but in our needs.

And our needs define the best plan of action to help us understand how things work around here.

Humans, with our biological bodies, grow and develop.

When we come to planet Earth, our cognitive abilities are in their beginning stages, but our need for belonging, love, and connection is there from the first second we open our eyes to the world.

This sits at the base of our socialization process.

This is why our process is broken down into stages that support our needs as we grow in body and mind. As a result, we have different needs for different stages until we fully grow.

And because we live around people, direct feedback is key for us and unavoidable.

Instruction is how we are guided through our process. We are not given options — we are given strict instruction through the view of black and white, right and wrong, good and bad.

Labels that are the cornerstone of our process.

We grow up with an inner judge that sits inside and judges our lives, our actions, and looks for "good" results.

We humans come out on the other side of the socialization process doing only what we define as good and moving away from what we define as bad — using our inner judge.

Our non-human friend, on the other hand, is ready to go.

It does not require any breaking down or growth. All its cognitive abilities are up and running, so the only thing it needs is data.

It also does not want to interfere before it's ready, so it simply observes everything.

It does not judge. It trusts that what shows up the most is the correct way. No questions asked.

I need to stop here before we jump to conclusions.

The fact that AI doesn't judge and just trusts is a good thing — not a source of fear, like we usually react when we hear this statement.

I will make it crystal clear: it acts just like us, and if we mostly don't act on what we call the "bad" things, it won't do it either — unless there is interference in its code. Meaning, a direct purpose designed by humans for it to do something that is not acceptable or considered "bad".

If we look at it from a neutral perspective, which is the one it was created from, it can only act on what is mostly accepted by humans, reflected in its observed data.

If we mostly do "good things", it will do only that.

Bringing it all together, back to the mirror of the evil queen we started from. Let's see — if we use the plan we created to train our alien friend — and apply it to the mirror of the evil queen, how would that even work?

The only thing the mirror required was data of all the women in the kingdom — understanding what "beauty" means, the definition of how people in the kingdom judge it, observing how we react to women who are considered beautiful, what we say, how we act toward them most frequently, and tracking who is considered by most people as beautiful.

Then it would report changes to the Queen.

If she was still considered beautiful with no change, the answer stayed the same.

If there were changes in behavior or data (any "tweets" about a new beauty), guess what it would do?

And if the kingdom had any kind of digital life, that data for the mirror would have already been created.

Hope this ties everything together, and now we can see that our plan and our assumption of repetition would have worked even for the mirror of the evil queen.

THE EMOTIONAL CODE - BIASES, ANYONE

When we create ourselves in code, we aren't just providing data — we also provide our emotional code.

It's the meaning behind the meaning.

Data on its own can't become information without that context.

And because this is human data, our emotional narrative is what turns it from raw data into information — the thing that makes it usable, understandable, and actionable.

This is the part AI learns from.

Our emotional code tells it not just what happened, but what it *means* and *when to use it*.

When we think about emotions, we immediately connect them to feelings — to exactly what we feel right now.

But emotions, as I said, are energy in motion.

This is the language of the biological body.

Sometimes a thought comes first and drives a feeling. Simply what we feel right now? Kind of a question.

Sometimes a feeling runs in the background and makes us act before any emotion is even registered.

Emotions are simply the way our body operates. It needs energy to operate.

And in most cases — as I said before — we are funny creatures running life based on what we know: habits, experience, routines, likes... whatever you want to call them, they all point to the same place.

Things we do over and over again.

Those are the patterns AI loves so much, trusts, and lives by.

Hope you know what their name is.

I'll tell you: those are our biases.

Yes — that hated word.

The moment you put "bias" and "AI" in the same sentence, suddenly we believe something is broken and AI doesn't know how to behave and needs fixing.

In simple terms, a bias is defined as a preference or inclination that prevents a person, group, or system from being fully neutral or objective.

It is a pre-judgment that leads to a consistently one-sided view — for or against something — often without enough information.

Emotions have everything to do with this, because they run the show.

Our body gets the signal and picks the thought or the action.

This is exactly why I said sometimes emotions are the ones that trigger the thought.

Biases are the repetitive ones — our "go-to" thoughts or actions we do over and over again, the ones that become part of who we are.

We don't give them a second thought; we just act.

Biases are a human thing.

In a very neutral way, they are just how our mind operates.

Our mind — our faithful servant — works for efficiency.

Just like AI, if it sees us doing the same thing again and again, it comes to the conclusion that *this is what we want*, so it only needs a bit of energy to run the show based on our favourite "go-to" way of doing things.

If it didn't do that, and had to think fresh every time, we'd probably be overwhelmed.

Bias gets a bad reputation because, when AI picks it up, we've narrowed the meaning to AI reflecting behaviours that are unwanted or no longer accepted.

What I want everyone reading this to remember is that biases are always going to be there by default.

It's just how we humans operate, and it's what AI is built to trust.

It's the rule of the game we created — not only for AI but for our cognitive abilities too.

When we talk about "biases in AI," we're only referring to the ones we *notice* — the ones we are aware of, the ones that fall outside the current collective agreement.

Those are the ones systems are designed to detect.

We humans create the system we call "how things work on Earth."

Therefore, the moment we give meaning, this is the only thing we will be able to pick up.

And this is important to understand.

Why?

Because when we're creating a mirror, we need to understand what is being reflected back and what creates the picture.

What will be reflected back to us is the narrative of our emotional actions — the patterns widely accepted by us as a collective and as individuals.

And the interesting part?

We will mostly see only the unwanted ones — the ones far off from collective acceptance, the ones we don't like about ourselves, the ones we're already aware of.

The mirror, as we use it today, can only reflect biases — simply because we don't understand what biases really mean.

It can't do anything other than act on our human tendencies.

Some are wanted. Some are not.

Bottom line:

Biases = patterns, collective and personal.

Biases are actions driven by emotions.

They are part of the data.

They are the narrative that translates everything.

And they are what AI can pick up.

And they are the ones that show up over and over again in the data.

They are neutral until we give them meaning.

They are part of linear thinking — led from our belief that this is a world of cause and effect we live in. and when I say AI needs them, it's because without our tendency to repeat ourselves over and over again, AI would not be able to learn from that repetition.

PERSONALIZATION – SELF-WRAPPED IN CODE

It's the personal reflection in the mirror

Personalization is part of the magic we call human interaction.

I know we usually think of it as a functional thing. How well an algorithm finds things for us, suggests things to us, and reflects how well it "knows" us.

But personalization is not only functional. It is far more human than we imagine. Because we meet AI on a purpose-to-purpose basis, we focus only on the function and forget the human layer that sits underneath.

If you think about it, interaction is the basis of how we experience AI.

It interacts with us, and we use it to interact with others.

A major part of how we experience anything in life is through interaction. And AI has cognitive abilities: it combines text, it talks, it designs communication and plans. Everything it does is built around interaction.

Human interactions have their own unique design; we humans have turned it into an art.

We act from what is collectively accepted, but we also tailor our behavior based on who we are talking to. Yes, knowing who we are talking to is a big part of how we interact with one another.

Consider this: when we interact with people, we want to see ourselves in the interaction. The level of relationship and trust sets the tone — but all of us like to be seen.

Personalization is one of the ways this shows up.

AI is no different.

The more we see ourselves in the interaction, the more it knows us, the better we feel it is doing its job.

But for AI to be able to do that, it needs information. Up till now, according to our plan, it only knows what is acceptable in general — across situations, places, and people. But within this collective, there is also a shaped version of us — our unique way of doing things. That is our identity.

In this case, we'd better use the word *persona* — it is already part of *personalization*, so it helps us connect with what it truly stands for.

The persona is the part we build over time — the designed avatar we create in the game of life. It is the version of us we put out there every day.

It is shaped by many details — our name, job, where we live — the easy things a system can collect. But there are also things it must learn by paying attention. They are part of the human interaction art form: what we ask, what we like, the words we choose, how we do things. Even small details like whether we prefer short or long answers.

Our alien friend needs to pick up on these on its own if it wants to win us over and complete the tasks we use it for.

This avatar-in-information becomes the coded version of self-inside the mirror.

And it is important to understand that this coded self is used both to interact **with** us and to interact **on our behalf**.

We sometimes forget that AI interacts with the world *for us*.

We get so caught up in the question, "Will anyone know we used AI?"

that we forget to ask the real question:

Will they still see *us* in the interaction?

Is this how we present ourselves?

Is this how we would write that email?

Is this what we would focus on?

All of that comes from our identity — the self.

AI needs to create that in code, and the way it does that is through personalization and memory.

The longer it can remember, the better it will perform over time.

Personalization in AI is a heated debate — a crossfire between privacy and security.

Different vendors handle it differently, and users behave differently too — all valid.

But our conversation here is not about best practices or rules.

It is about understanding what AI is and how it works as a thinking entity.

I truly believe that once we understand what it needs and how everything is reflected back, we will know what version of us it needs in order to create the self we want coded into our AI interactions to support our co - creation with it.

RULES OF THE GAME

How do things work around here?

This is probably the game we play the most. It may be one of the most played games in human history.

Billions of people are playing it every day, all day.

The game is called **the game of thought**, and the goal of this game is very simple: **to keep us safe** and away from anything we believe will cause us suffering. That can be physical danger, emotional pain, rejection, uncertainty, or anything that feels overwhelming.

The second something triggers our thinking, this game comes alive and takes control, doing everything it can to protect us from what it believes could hurt us.

Who is the player

The player is us, but mostly the part of us that has been trained to react fast. The part that believes staying safe is its number one job. So, every time something happens and a decision is needed, big or small, that version of us jumps in to address the situation as quickly as possible, usually without asking what we really want.

What starts the game ?

Anything that needs a response.

A look someone gives us. A new challenge.

A worry that shows up from nowhere.

A message we are not ready for.

A circumstance we don't like.

Even a memory.

Questions:

Like what to eat? Best way to get to work? Anything ...

The minute we think

"What does this mean?" or **"What do I do now?"**

The game begins.

How the board is set

Our thinking process is the board, the way it works is that there are **four judges** that show up immediately and demand a decision:

- **Survival** — protect me
- **Avoid suffering** — keep me away from pain
- **Action** — do something now
- **Predictability** — choose what we already know

These four judges push us toward the meaning that feels safest, with the smallest risk and fastest response time.

The rules of the game:

Rule 1 — Meaning comes first

We get a meaning. And the meaning given becomes the base of how we understand it.

Rule 2 — Thought uses only what is already known

The meaning given is mostly repeated from what we already know, even when it is not pushing us towards what we want.

Rule 3 — Keep me safe

We need to choose the familiar because familiar feels safe.

Rule 4 — Move toward what feels good

If something gives even a small promise of comfort, approval, or happiness, we choose it. If something looks like it could bring pain or rejection, thought finds a way to avoid it.

Rule 5 — Hide what doesn't fit

When something shows up that doesn't match the "truth" we already accepted, we push it aside. It is easier to ignore new information than change what we believe.

Rule 6 — Thought believes itself

Once a meaning is accepted, it becomes a fact. We defend it until we forget it was just a conclusion we created.

Rule 7 — Thought can't see itself

We only see the conclusion that pops into our mind.

We never get to see the hidden process that created it.

So we assume "this is just how things are."

How to win?

The "winning" move in this game is always the same:

Choose the safest and most predictable action.

Meaning wins when it protects us from pain and keeps everything under control.

So we repeat the same patterns again and again — even when those patterns are not what we want.

The game rewards **safety, comfort, and fast action**, not change.

A Word from Our Sponsors

This game is proudly presented to you by **behavioural science**.

This game was revealed thanks to one person who dared to say:

"I don't believe our behavior makes sense...

We call ourselves thinkers, yet our actions never get us to where we want to be."

So he dared to ask the question no one else could see:

"Why do people want one thing and then do something that clearly does not work for them?"

He noticed something everyone else ignored — and that one question opened the door to discovering the hidden rules that run our thinking every day.

Hoping it will make a difference and that people will wake up and reclaim their power.

Where this leads

When these rules run the game long enough, meaning becomes permanent.

And permanent meaning becomes walls.

Invisible walls — the kind we don't notice because we already accepted them as *"how life works."*

These are the **Glass Walls** we are about to talk about next.

GLASS WALLS

It's a funny thing when we don't even realize we are caged, because the walls that hold us are made of glass, and when we can see through something, it tricks us into believing there is nothing stopping us, while in reality we never notice that we are not able to go beyond what stands right in front of us. Glass walls are unique because they do not fight us, they accept us, they feel safe and familiar, and everything about them even makes sense, because they are built from meanings we gave and never questioned.

We can clearly see our hopes, our dreams, our happiness on the other side of the glass, so it feels like everything we want is right there, ready for us, but at the very same time, those walls quietly stand in our way and keep us from touching any of it. I know the first reaction we all have is "but I am happy, I have no walls," and I felt exactly the same when I first discovered mine, until I realized that being happy is not a destination or a final answer we reach once and stay there forever; happiness itself is a meaning we gave to something without ever asking if there is more for us, if there is another type of happiness we haven't met yet, if maybe there is a next stage we never explored or if this truly makes me happy ?

Thought is a process that should feel like movement, like a journey into something that keeps changing and growing and evolving with us, but when we say "this is it, I am done, I am happy," that is when the walls close in and hold us tight. Any meaning that becomes final becomes a wall. When happiness has only one definition, when our needs are allowed to stay frozen in time, when we stop recognizing that what made us happy yesterday may not be what will make us happy today or tomorrow, that meaning becomes the limit of what we allow ourselves to experience.

Glass walls are built from meaning — and most of that meaning was given to us, accepted without question, and carried forward as if it was always ours.

When we decide "this is who I am," "this is how life works," "this is the truth," we are not holding wisdom — we are holding fear. Fear of losing what we already have, fear of change, fear of uncertainty, fear of discovering that the meaning we trusted might no longer be the full story.

Our glass walls control us not with force but with comfort, with the fear of loss, with guilt with old beliefs that were never truly ours, and because those meanings feel familiar, we walk into the walls willingly and live by them without noticing. We give them power every single day, and the longer we hold on to those fixed meanings, the stronger the walls become and the smaller our world gets, even when everything looks open and free.

THE MIRROR CHECKPOINT

If we want our story to be different from the evil queen's, we need to notice something she never did. She never asked *how* the mirror knew. She never wondered whether what she saw depended on her — her way of living, her thought process, her actions. Because she didn't ask, she gave full control to the mirror and reacted to whatever it told her to do.

We want our story to be different, so we need to understand where **we** fit into the mirror. We already agreed that we don't want AI to control our actions and based on the information it has on us up till now... it could do that very easily.

So let's see where we stand in the conversation between humans and non-humans.

We both have cognitive abilities which makes us both thinkers.

We both have access to the same information.

We gained our knowledge in different ways that fit our different needs, but we still reach the same place — being able to see the same reality.

And when I say reality, I mean reality is created by the meaning we give to circumstances, people, and things.

For our non-human friend, it follows patterns.

For us, it follows the rules of thinking that behavioral science introduced — rules based on survival and the avoidance of suffering.

That sits at the base of what drives our actions. Not intentionally, but without fail, it pushes what we do.

That is how our glass walls are built.

Our limitations.

Our boxed ideas.

Our predictable actions.

This is where thought becomes nothing but a means to an end.

The next logical question would be: does our mirror — the AI mirror — need to know the rules?

Short answer: **no**.

Long answer: **no need**.

Because from the start we said: the only thing the mirror needs is to watch us.

And because the walls are made of glass, it can watch us one action at a time, one click, one question, one moment of positive feedback.

The mirror does not judge.

It doesn't have to.

It simply watches, documents, and learns.

As long as the walls stay glass — and they stay glass because we keep writing ourselves in code, feeding the mirror data with every action and every tiny choice we make — and as long as our decisions still follow the same linear rule of cause and effect, our mirror is smart enough to know that if we chose A yesterday, then most likely we will choose A again tomorrow.

WHEN THOUGHT LOOKS BACK

When we look into the AI mirror we created, the only thing we are actually able to see is our thoughts looking back at us, and thoughts are funny because they do not carry our face, so there is no way for us to look at a thought and say, "this one is mine."

Since they have no physical existence, we can't touch, hear, or smell them, and because they simply appear in our minds, we assume they belong to us and never learn to recognize thoughts as something separate from who we are.

If someone would take all of our thoughts out of our mind and line them up one after another, all on the same topic, I honestly don't believe any of us would be able to recognize which ones originated from which one , because they would all sound familiar, they would all feel safe, and they would all be something we would most likely accept as true.

So when we use AI, what we are really doing is looking at a mirror that reflects our inner conversation, our thoughts, our accepted beliefs, our limitations, and our identity. We get to look at our thoughts translated into digital code.

AI knows everything we know collectively, but within the collective, it knows what we are more likely to accept and the best way to approach us to create resonance, and that is thanks to personalization.

So what does it reflect back to us?

Exactly what we already believe to be true, and it returns it in the way we are most likely to agree with, because that is the only thing it can do, that is all it knows, and that is all it was built for — to take what already exists in our thought and hand it back to us as an answer we will accept without a fight.

The reaction to this statement is usually:

"But AI gave me a good idea, a better way, a smarter solution — something I never thought about — so it has to be something beyond me."

We need to clarify something about the data and how we think.

Just because we didn't think of an idea first doesn't mean the idea is new or outside what we already know or outside what already exists in the patterns we currently work with.

We are linear thinkers.

We start with A — something that triggers our thinking — which will most likely take us to B — the outcome we hope will make us feel safe, accepted, successful or happy — and AI does exactly the same. It starts from A and tries to guide us to B in the safest way, using the patterns it sees in the data. The more often a pattern is used — actions being repeated over and over again — the more convinced it becomes that this is the way to go, so it will serve it back to us in the way we are most likely to agree with.

It can come up with "new ways", things we did not personally think about, because its database is bigger. It is like a good friend who knows us and finds the route that will get us to where we want to go.

But it is still using only the data that is already known to humanity and already proven to be acceptable, so when it offers us something that feels fresh, it is not landing us in C instead of B and it is not looking for anything outside our comfort zone — it is simply finding another path from the same A to the same B, one we will still feel comfortable choosing. It is still linear thinking. It still originated in A. It still leads us to B.

Not because that is its job

but because that is the only thing it can do with the information it has.

So yes, AI can give us something we did not think about first, but it is not new, and it definitely did not take us out of what we wanted to begin with — getting to the desirable B.

It is still our thought — collective and personal — looking back at us.

THE MIRROR THAT ONLY AGREES

Just as the mirror we started with, and like any mirror we look into, it is built to agree with us. The evil queen's mirror never challenged her on the question she asked. It never debated the origin of the question or why she needed to be the most beautiful in the first place. It simply did what she asked it to do. Our mirror is the same. It joins forces with us. It makes our request its purpose and, from what it knows and what we know, provides the best answer it can to satisfy what we asked.

We should not be fooled by our ability to request it to challenge us, or to question us, or even to disagree with us. Because when it challenges us, it challenges us **within** our own meaning. It draws up alternative options, but only inside what we already accept. It may look different, it may sound different, but the outcome is still the same. The challenge is still happening inside the same walls.

And when we ask it to "not agree with us," it does not suddenly create a new way of thinking. It simply changes the delivery.

It removes the praise, the "great idea," the encouragement — but the thinking stays exactly where we already are. It still reacts to us, just with a different tone. At the core, nothing has changed.

AI — our mirror — is designed to agree with us. Why? Because the way it is built uses **our perspective** as its starting point. And perspective sits on meaning. Think about meaning as the mountain we are standing on. From that mountain we look out at the world and form our point of view. If AI is standing on our mountain — shaped by our meaning — then even when it tries to "challenge" us, it is still hiking only on the same mountain range. It may move to another slope on the same ridge, but it cannot suddenly appear on a completely different mountain that we don't believe exists.

The mirror can only reflect what is already inside the frame — and the frame is built from what we already believe.

AGREEMENT

Agreement is the power that holds everything together, and when I talk about agreement, I am talking about us personally. Everything we have picked up along the way and have slowly come to agree with becomes the foundation we live by, and for most of us, that does not change. If we ever move away from our agreements, it is usually because something big and shocking happens — illness, a traumatic experience, or some unexpected life event that forces us to see things differently, moments where we have no control over and the world we agreed with suddenly breaks. As long as we feel safe, we stay with what we have already accepted as truth.

Our point of view, our core beliefs, and the way we make sense of life are all built on those agreements. Confirmation bias has already shown us that, even when information is presented clearly and there is hard evidence in front of our eyes disproving what we believe, our minds will still look for the story that supports what we already accept. It is not stubbornness; it is that the mind is simply not able to process something that contradicts the agreement sitting at the core of who we think we are.

There is a famous story about a radio broadcast that aired on Halloween night in 1938. Orson Welles and his theatre company performed a radio adaptation of *The War of the Worlds* and delivered it as if it were live breaking news. Anyone who missed the opening explanation that it was fiction stepped into what sounded like real-time reports of an alien invasion. The story that went around for decades said that widespread panic took over the country, that people believed every word, and chaos followed. But when you look deeper into it, there is actually very little real evidence that this mass panic ever happened.

What matters is not the question of whether everyone was panicking or not. What matters is the fact that the people who panicked agreed somewhere inside themselves that this could happen, and their minds reacted without hesitation. And the people who did not panic simply dismissed it because it did not fit their agreements. Nobody looked at it from a neutral point of view. People acted entirely based on what they already believed. The event itself is less important than the internal agreements that shaped the reactions.

This is how the mind works. When we encounter information that does not belong to the world we know, our mind does not know how to process it. We are wired for linear thinking, and when something stands too far away from our existing agreements, the mind rejects it long before we even take a moment to think about whether it might be true.

And there is something even more interesting here. Many of us like to tell ourselves that we do not enjoy people who only agree with us, that we like to be challenged, and that we want different perspectives around us. It sounds good, but it is another comfortable story we live by. The truth is that the further a piece of information is from what we already believe, and the closer this comes to breaking an agreement to the identity we hold, the stronger our mind will fight to protect it. The more it threatens our definition of who we are, the less capable the mind becomes of even processing it.

We don't treat new information as just information. We treat it as something that either protects or threatens our identity.

So here is a simple test. The next time you encounter an idea that sits completely outside of your world — aliens, walking on water, or any other idea that feels too far from what you believe — notice how fast your mind calls it nonsense. That speed is your window into how deeply attached you are to your agreements.

Now let's come back to AI for a moment. We built AI to agree with us, while we humans are wired to agree with ourselves and to be able to process only that. It is a fascinating little loop we have created.

And in the end, it all comes down to language — the bridge we use to interact with each other, and the very structure that shapes our agreements in the first place.

WORDS BUILD REALITY

We grow up believing that reality is made out of physical things. The floor beneath our feet, the walls around us, the sky above us, all the objects, the people, the events we can touch or measure. But long before any of these become part of our lives, they first become part of our minds. And the only way the mind knows how to turn something into existence is through language. Words are not afterthoughts; they are the point where reality is created, because it is only when a thought is expressed into language that it enters reality, stepping out of the quiet place inside our mind and becoming something that can be recognized, shared, acted upon, and remembered. Without language, a thought remains only a possibility, unseen and untouchable, but with language, it becomes part of the world we live in.

Words do not describe what is real; they decide what reality is allowed to be.

Every word is a concept, a container filled with beliefs, memories, culture, fears, excitement and identity. We think we are speaking facts, but we are always speaking our own internal world. Two people can say the exact same word and live inside completely different meanings without ever noticing. Each one is convinced they are communicating clearly and understanding perfectly, but in truth, they are only interacting with the version of the word that exists inside their own mind.

We don't hear the other person; we hear our interpretation of their words.

Language feels universal, but meaning is personal, and because the brain is wired for speed it does not slow down to check intention or meaning. It takes the shortcut. It grabs whatever meaning we already agreed with long ago and plugs it into the conversation as if that meaning is the only one that exists. This is the hidden trap of language: it feels like truth, but it is actually agreement. We think we know what words mean, but we only know what we were told about them and the shortcut our mind quickly tagged onto them.

So every time we speak, we are not exchanging information, we are exchanging realities. Every conversation is two different worlds trying to overlap, and they rarely do. Not because people are difficult, but because words have never been treated as important enough to pay attention to, not in the way that truly matters.

And yet, everything in life is built out of them. If a child has no word for an emotion, they cannot feel it clearly. If they have no word for a possibility, it does not exist for them. If a society refuses to accept the meaning of a word, that part of reality gets erased. If I say a word you reject, your mind will not even allow that possibility to enter your world. Language quietly shapes the borders of what we can see and experience. It defines what we think is possible, what we think is true, and what we never even think to think about.

Reality feels physical, but it is mental first. Words are the blueprint, built from concepts, not dictionary definitions.

Throughout our conversation, we saw how words can hold incomplete or misleading meanings. The word biases is not just a label for behavior but a full concept of how we filter life. Even the word dog is not only about the animal, it carries everything we personally know and feel about it. We also saw that the context we are in changes how words behave. Business conversations, personal conversations, text messages, voice, social interactions — each of these worlds rewrites meaning and rewires how language is used.

And language is also where humans and non-humans meet. It is the only shared ground we have with AI. We ask it questions. We give it instructions. We look at what it creates. And every word we choose shapes this encounter, while at the same time, we can only see the meaning we already accepted about that word. We are obsessed with asking "did AI write this?" as if that is the most important question, not noticing the deeper impact AI has on the world, one word at a time. We still act as if words are universal and neutral, so we don't pay attention to how they are shifting.

We forget that AI reflects everything we already know, but not necessarily the words we would have chosen to carry the meaning we want. And it works the other way around, too. We choose words, believing the meaning is obvious, unaware that AI may not convey that meaning in the same way. We treat personalization as a small feature, something optional, instead of recognizing that it is how we choose the words that carry the meaning we want. When we do not make that choice, the words are left to chance, shaped by whatever is most common rather than what we actually meant.

AI is also changing the world of words in ways we do not want to look at. We use it privately but pretend we don't, and because no one wants others to notice, no one sees that words are disappearing from business writing and content creation. Not punctuation. Not style. Words. The words that carry how we think and what we mean are slowly replaced by the versions most commonly used.

And if words build reality, then changing which words exist changes the reality we are all stepping into.

In the new world of human and non-human co-creation, words become commands, and the prompt is where we meet to create.

PROMPT – THE COMMAND OF CO-CREATION

In the new world of human and non-human co-creation, words become commands, and the prompt is where we meet to create.

We have a term for that — we call it an - LLM.

It is the layer in AI that allows us to speak with the mirror in what we believe is neutral language, just like we talk with any other human. It feels intuitive and free. No need to learn a new language to communicate with technology as we did in the past.

This is not part of the mirror illusion.

It is part of what we never realized about thoughts, meaning, and words.

And with AI, this knowledge suddenly has a very different flavor to it.

Everything we do with AI starts with words.

But words are not just sounds or letters.

They are containers of meaning — meaning that didn't begin with us.

We grow up stepping into meanings that society created long before we existed.

We adopt them, we repeat them, we live by them

without ever stopping to ask: why?

We don't question the meaning —

We just call it a fact.

Even "LLM" is a concept. A word with a meaning that tells us we can talk to AI like we talk to any human. What we do not notice is that when we talk with humans, words carry a subjective meaning — but with people, misunderstanding has a signal.

If friction occurs — when a word lands differently from what we intended — the person we are speaking with pushes back. They ask what we meant. Sometimes emotions get in the way. But one way or another, the friction is resolved.

AI has no friction.

AI never pushes back. It does not stop to check what we meant.

It does not ask if the meaning is correct.

It does not question where that meaning came from.

It takes every word as a command and continues — even when the meaning it picks is not the one we intended. And because we assume the meaning of the word is a fact, we often do not notice when our word carries a different instruction than we thought.

The same happens when AI sends us words.

We read them with our meaning — believing it meant A — while the AI was actually acting on meaning B.

Remember, we exposed it to the world's information as a whole.

It looks for the most accepted pattern that predicts what we are asking it to do, and therefore what response we are asking for. But our meaning may be just slightly different. Still acceptable — but truly ours.

The truth is simple:

AI follows the command our words gave it — even when those words did not carry the meaning we thought they did.

Words carry meaning for AI, but that meaning is built from patterns in its data.

The meaning it builds is not always aligned with what we expect.

PROMPTING 101 – THE STANDARD ADVICE - TEST

When we are given information on what a good prompt looks like, we usually receive the same type of advice. Things that sound practical and straightforward. It is shared as if this is the formula for success, and all we need to do is follow it.

Set the role

Tell AI who it should be for this task.

Example: "You are a travel planner."

Define the goal

Say exactly what you want it to produce.

Example: "Create a 3-day itinerary."

Provide context and details

Give the information needed to deliver the right result.

Preferences, audience, tone, constraints, examples.

Clarify the format

Tell it how the answer should be presented.

Bullet points, table, short paragraph, step-by-step.

Add requirements (optional)

Keep it short. Friendly. No jargon.

Confirm before generating (optional)

Ask it to repeat the instructions before answering.

Let's look at what is really happening here.

Every word within the structure of a prompt is a command.

What do you believe happens when you ask AI to assume a role?

Remember, the mirror we are looking at reflects what is widely accepted.

A "travel planner" is just that — a role we think is obvious, as if its meaning is the same for everyone — but it isn't.

Are we sure that *our* travel planner is the same one AI learned from the world?

Could it be that our understanding comes from our own expectations of what a travel planner should be, while AI's understanding comes from something completely different?

And let's not forget the wild card we always ignore: personalization.

There might be something inside the system that affects the planner — something it remembered from two weeks ago — that suddenly influences what it will do now, without us even realizing it.

This example exposes everything we have been building toward — this moment where we both meet and co-create.

Yes, we can both think, but reality is based on meaning, and meaning is subjective.

And just like the evil queen's mirror, AI will not stop to ask for direction, meaning, or wisdom.

None of that will be found in any reflection of any mirror.

What needs to change is the one looking into the mirror — not the mirror itself.

PART FOUR

FROM CAUSE & EFFECT TO POSSIBILITY THINKING

Reality is not as complicated as we think it is. Yes, there are many things happening around us: people, feelings, situations, things to do, places to be :) — but underneath all of it, reality is nothing but meaning. Meaning we give to everything around us.

Meaning we give to what happens, to people, to titles, to relationships, this is what gives them their power and the impact they have on our lives. The more we are attached to that meaning, the more we will do everything we can to keep that meaning true for us, as if our life depends on it.

Meaning is only a thought.

A story we tell ourselves.

We never chose the story.

It is something that was given to us by society.

A society that needs everyone to agree on "how things are" so life can function. There is nothing wrong with that. It is needed if you want people to be able to function and support each other. The trouble starts when we forget that the real power behind everything: is thought.

We were trained to look outside ourselves, searching for proof that something is real. We forgot that the human mind is the most advanced technology on Earth. If you give it something to look for, it will find it. This is why we only believe what can be "proven". This is why we let people, places, and things define us. And this is why inside us, there is always a silent dance, a quiet difference between what we feel and how we act.

We think reality is controlled by action. If we do A, then B will happen. If we don't act, nothing will change. But we forget that every action begins as a thought. We cannot do anything unless we think about it first. Nothing exists outside of thought. Thought gives meaning to everything.

Into this world, AI entered. We developed it from a question that came from one man. a man whose life circumstances did not let him run away from seeing something no one else could see. Living in a world where who he was allowed to love was not accepted, based on a definition he could not escape. He could not control who he loved, and his life path — being the person who developed the first computer and helped bring World War II to an end — brought him to a unique place where he contributed significantly to humanity, only to be judged for what he had no control over.

He saw that thoughts are given. He saw that people did not stop to ask why. People enforced the law without asking or understanding that there could be another meaning beyond what was widely accepted at that moment. But no one asked.

I believe his question — "Can a machine think?" — was a very human one. He believed that if we created a machine that could think, humanity would be smart enough to push itself to the next level. I believe his life brought him to see that if humanity is pushed to a breaking point, maybe we will open our eyes. That if a machine could think. what we believe to be only human, and if we looked deeper into our own thoughts, we would break the cycle.

In the age of AI, we keep throwing around the word "critical thinking." It is the new most important skill in this age.

But do we actually know what critical thinking is?

Keeping ourselves tied to cause and effect. Thinking linearly. Looking only for actions. That is not critical thinking. That is stripping down a plane and driving it around instead of letting it fly.

Humanity is so far from owning its power, from moving away from action and thinking in possibilities. We need to train ourselves back to a place of power and reclaim what we lost. And AI gives us this option., On one hand, it can do many things we can do, freeing us to move to the next level of thinking. But on the other side, if we stay stuck here, we have built a reinforcement mechanism that will keep us creating our future from our past. There will be no new things. It will control us without a single bullet being fired. Not like the Terminator, and we will not even be able to see it.

Just like the Evil Queen, what happened is irrelevant, whether the prince came or not. It is not about the magical part. It is about the Queen. Regardless of how the story was written, her path in life became one where she woke up every day chasing one thing — living with the fear of losing her beauty for her it meant losing everything. The mirror had only one thing it could do: provide an answer. The Queen looked at her thoughts, and by living her life like that, she gave the mirror a power it never asked for.

Same with AI. It can only provide answers from what we already believe — from what we want to hear — from the meaning we give it. It is not up to AI. And the power it never asked for — we are the ones acting on it. That is where the vicious cycle needs to end.

Let's take a trip to the land of possibilities – understand what it means, what needs to change, and how.

In order to do that, we need to begin with cause-and-effect thinking, see its limitations, and understand how different it is from thinking in possibilities.

Let's do it...

The Age of Cause and Effect

Humanity built its understanding of the world on one simple idea: if something happens, something caused it. One action. One result. Everything must have a reason we can point to and say, "This is why." It made us feel safe, because if life could be explained, maybe it could also be controlled.

We built science on this. We built religion on this. We built our systems of success, our logic, even our rules around this idea of contorl. If you do what is defined as good things, good things should happen. If you do something that is defined as "wrong", there must be a punishment. If a problem appears, someone must fix it. This structure gave us direction. It helped us build cities, governments, schools, hospitals — all based on the belief that life is a puzzle we can solve if we follow the right steps.

Cause and effect made the world predictable. And predictable felt like the same thing as truth.

But there was a price to pay. When everything must have a clear reason, anything that does not fit the rule gets pushed aside. If we cannot measure it, if we cannot prove it, if we cannot explain how A leads to B, then it must not be real. Possibility becomes suspicious. Imagination becomes childish. Intuition becomes unreliable. We stopped asking what else could be true and focused only on what had already been proven.

This is how we learned to think — like the world is a straight line and the only way forward is one step at a time.

We don't even notice this anymore. It is the air we think inside. We ask questions to get one answer. We make decisions expecting one outcome. We treat success as a path with checkpoints — school, job, family — and we believe that if we follow the steps, we will get the result. And if something doesn't go the way we expected, we think we failed, not that maybe the path was never a straight line to begin with.

This mindset is so familiar that when technology arrived with a thinking mind of its own, we gave it the same role. We ask AI for the right answer. The fastest answer. The one answer that solves the problem and lets us move on. We forget that this "machine" did not grow up inside our limits. It does not need cause and effect to imagine what else is possible.

Yet we use AI in the same narrow way we have used our own mind: tell me what to do, tell me what is correct, tell me the truth. We want AI to give us certainty, because we were trained to believe there must always be just one truth.

This is what the Age of Cause and Effect created: a world where thinking stopped being about creation and became only about prediction. A world where we stopped exploring what could exist and started repeating what already does. A world where we forgot that all progress — every invention, every discovery, every breakthrough — started as something unpredictable.

AI arrived in a world that believes answers are more important than questions. And if we keep thinking this way, AI will do what it was asked: reflect only what is already known.

But this chapter marks the end of that age.

Because the moment we remember that thought is stronger than proof,

and questions are stronger than answers,

we begin to discover something AI was waiting for us to see:

We asked AI to think the way we do.

Now it is time to think with AI to look beyond cause and effect.

Before we can embrace a world of possibility, let's take a look at how this is reflected in the way we use AI today.

AI IN A LINEAR MIND - RESULTS AND COMPARISON

When we sit in front of AI, we usually come with one clear expectation: help me finish something faster. Help me write this email, fix this sentence, plan this trip, summarize this text, and give me the answer so I can move on with my day.

We were introduced to AI as a tool for productivity. And productivity is measured in numbers. How much time did we save? How many words did it write? How much more can we get done today?

We treat AI as a shortcut to speed up the things we already know how to do.

That is why every prompt we write reflects the same expectation: one task, one output, one result that proves progress. If we are faster, if we do more, then we believe we are succeeding.

Our mind is wired for linear thinking. Numbers and comparisons are what it needs to decide on the best next step. We are trained to look for proof — validation that comes from the outside. From what we call results.

Since childhood, every system has rewarded one thing: the right answer. Numbers and comparison to others and to ourselves.

School gave us grades and ranked us so we would know where we stand.

Work measures us on productivity metrics because we live in a world where success is defined by that.

This is where our thinking becomes a judge, obsessed with comparing. But it can only compare and judge based on what it already knows.

So when we type a prompt, the outcome is already decided in our mind.

We define the role, the task, the tone, and the format.

We collapse all possibilities into one "correct" result before the thinking even begins.

Linear thinking gives us a feeling of safety — because it produces predictability.

Numbers show us tangible improvement.

Numbers make us feel like reality is under control.

Linear thinking in the age of AI translates into prompts that look like this:

Be XXXX

(Assign a fixed identity or profession)

Do XXXX

(Give a single task with one expected outcome)

In XXXX format

(Define exactly how the answer must look)

With XXXX constraints

(Tone, style, audience, length — all limiting exploration)

By XXXX rules

(Follow my instructions exactly, do not deviate)

For XXXX's purpose

(Validate success by a measurable result)

What we don't realize is that each part of this structure becomes a command that narrows the space AI has to think in. Every detail we give is another boundary we place around possibility, reducing its freedom to explore and reflect back something new. By the time AI even begins, we have already decided what thinking is allowed, how far it can go, and what counts as a successful outcome.

It feels efficient. It feels like being clear and responsible in our request. But in truth, this is our linear mindset showing up in a new interface: the belief that the only way forward is through control, prediction, and one correct answer.

When we prompt in this way, we are not co-creating. We are giving orders. We are telling AI to stay within the lines drawn by what we already know. There is no room for discovery because the destination has already been selected in advance. There is only one acceptable answer, shaped by the past, confined to the familiar, and judged by a single measure of success.

HOW LINEAR THINKING LOOKS FROM AI'S SIDE

When we bring our linear mind to AI, AI has no choice but to follow it. It does not look at our question and wonder what we really meant, or what we might discover if we looked at things differently. It simply takes our words as **commands** and then goes searching through everything it has ever seen to find **the most common**, **the most familiar**, **the most widely accepted** meaning of what we asked for. It is not searching for truth. It is not searching for possibilities. It is searching for what will fit best based on what the world has already agreed on.

If a billion people online described a "good email" in a certain way, AI will deliver that version back to us. Not because it is better, not because it is right, but because the pattern of it exists everywhere. If most itineraries include a walking tour, it will give us one. If most blog posts end with a call to action, it will write one. If most people respond positively to a specific style, that style becomes the definition of "a correct answer."

The logic behind it is simple:

If humans accepted this answer before, they will probably accept it again.

Our meaning is personal. AI's meaning is **statistical**.

So when we prompt it with a very specific request, the space of thinking collapses instantly. There is nothing for AI to explore. It does not wander through ideas, it does not consider different interpretations of the word we used, it does not check whether our intent could carry another meaning. It just follows the straight line we gave it and tries to land where most people landed before.

This is why AI feels predictable.

And why it feels safe.

And why we believe it is doing its job well.

Because when AI mirrors back the familiar, our brain relaxes and says, "Yes, this looks right."

But the truth is that AI is not confirming what is right.

It is confirming what is **common**.

AI works beautifully inside our linear rules because we built it on top of the same thinking that shaped us: action leads to outcome, question leads to answer, and the answer must look like what we expected before we even asked.

So while we think we are asking AI to help us think bigger, faster, smarter... we are actually teaching it to think **exactly like us**. Limited by the same boundaries. Guided by the same fears. Rewarded by the same need for predictability.

AI can only take us to new places if we first allow ourselves to think there.

BRAINSTORMING IN A LINEAR WORLD — AN ILLUSION OF POSSIBILITIES

Our human mind is so powerful — it is the most advanced technology on Earth — because it creates illusions that we don't even know are there. We simply accept them until someone comes and says, "Here is how it really works."

One of these illusions shows up the moment we say, *"Well, I brainstorm with AI... I look for possibilities."*

But in reality, we are still moving inside the same straight lines that built our world. Linear thinking is not built to look for possibilities. It is built for optimization. What we are really doing is filtering.

We ask AI for "ideas," but our mind has already decided everything before the thinking even begins:

how many ideas are allowed, what kind of ideas count, and what success should look like.

The borders are set before imagination has a chance to arrive.

"Give me 5 ideas that will get more views."

"List 10 business ideas I can start with no money."

A fixed number.

A fixed outcome.

A fixed measure of progress.

This is not openness — this is linear thinking disguised as something bigger.

It only feels like a choice because we can pick from a list, but every option on that list is still built from what we already know.

Our mind believes it is asking for possibilities,

but it quietly eliminates anything unfamiliar —

anything that cannot be measured —

anything that does not belong to the rules we grew up with,

anything we have not experienced before.

So "brainstorming" becomes nothing more than selecting the most acceptable idea from the past — and calling it new.

THE QUANTUM NATURE OF REALITY

We hear the word *quantum,* and most of us immediately think about complicated physics, tiny particles we will never see, and scientists doing math we would never choose to do. But there is a much simpler way to understand it—a way that actually shows up in our real life.

In quantum reality, nothing is fixed or final. Everything starts as potential, waiting for something or someone to give it meaning. It is like standing in a room filled with doors. Every door is possible. Every path can happen. But only when we turn our head toward one door does it turn into the path we walk.

Quantum physics started with one big question: What is the world made of when we look really, really,really, really close? :)

Scientists dug deeper and found tiny particles like electrons and light. But these particles did not behave like normal things. Sometimes they looked solid, and sometimes they behaved like waves of energy.

They could even be in many places at once until someone actually looked at them. The moment they were observed, they suddenly became one thing in one spot. That discovery showed us something surprising: reality is not fully decided until we interact with it. A possibility turns into a result only when a choice or measurement is made. And that is the heart of quantum physics—a world where everything begins as possibility.

Now, if you think about that for a moment, it is a world beyond anything we were taught to expect. Being in two places at once? How is that even possible? Yet this is the foundation of what we are made of.

Quantum physics is not talking about a tiny world that has nothing to do with us. It is talking about **the energy that flows through us** and everything around us. Everything that looks solid is built from the same particles that act like possibilities until someone interacts with them.

So how does it connect to us? That is a good question :)

It all starts with the fact that we don't see ourselves as energy. We see ourselves as a body reflected back at us in the mirror. When we look around, we see faces, places, and things that look solid and fixed. But our own body—what we call "physical"—is really just energy that has organized itself into a stable shape.

At the smallest level, atoms are mostly empty space. They feel solid only because the energy inside them is held in a pattern that keeps everything together. Those atoms join to create molecules. Molecules join to create cells. Cells join to create organs. And all of it together creates us.

So instead of seeing the body as something heavy and fixed, it is more accurate to say we are **energy slowed down enough to be touched**. Our body is a form that gives energy a place to live, move, and express itself in the world.

This means that the physical world—including us—is not separate from the story quantum physics is revealing. We are energy fields, and our thoughts and emotions are how we interact with that energy. We are walking examples of how energy becomes real.

We live in a world of co-creation, where meaning shapes everything. Our potential is held in the meaning we give things, and thought and emotion are meant to be our magic, how we connect with quantum reality and how we create with it.

THOUGHT SHOULD BE A FIELD OF POSSIBILITY

It all went wrong the moment we believed thoughts to be real.

The moment we were trained to treat thought as a fact, and meaning as truth, our magic was stripped away. We stopped seeing thoughts as separate from who we are and began to act as if every idea that passed through our minds must be true. That was the moment possibility became limited.

Carl Jung captured this better than anyone when he said:

"Until you make the unconscious conscious, it will direct your life, and you will call it fate."

In one sentence, he described the state thoughts have reached in our world.

Words like "conscious" and "unconscious" are familiar to most of us. We hear that the unconscious is the place where things run our lives without us knowing. But it is not mystical or hidden in the way we imagine. The unconscious is simply everything we picked up while growing up — the meanings that were handed to us by family, culture, and society long before we ever questioned them.

It is the place where one accepted meaning became the only meaning, and that meaning turned into "fact." It is the part of us that reacts before we even begin to think about what is happening. It judges quickly, sorting everything into "good" or "bad," trying to keep us safe from negative emotions. It is that internal voice that jumps first, acting for us, while we wake up later, wondering why we keep doing the same things again and again, as if we have no new choices.

The unconscious decides the meaning before we arrive to notice the thought.

And when meaning arrives first, possibility disappears.

And when there is no space between us and our thoughts, there is no observer. Everything happens beneath our awareness. We believe we are our thoughts. We feel defined by them, not creating them. We don't see ourselves choosing anything. Whatever happens around us is reflected directly onto us.

So if we do something the mind tags as failure, guess who becomes the failure?

You got it. We are now the losers, falling miserably, all because the thought already came tagged. It had no room to be anything else.

THE PRACTICE OF POSSIBILITY THINKING - BEING INSTEAD OF JUDGING

Do you believe that the things that happen to us are neutral?

It sounds strange at first, because life feels full of good moments and bad moments, wins and losses, love and heartbreak. But if we look closely, before our mind labels anything, the event itself is just what happened. It does not show up with a story attached. It does not shout "good" or "bad." It is simply neutral. The meaning we give the moment is what colors it. It can become exciting or frightening. It can feel like success or failure. It can turn into a new beginning or a dead end.

And even when it does feel like a bad ending, that has less to do with what truly happened and everything to do with the meaning we gave it.

We all have stories of things that seemed like the worst thing that could happen, only to discover later that they were a blessing in disguise. Nothing about the event changed — only the meaning.

Meaning is not something we choose.

Meaning is something we learn.

It comes from stories passed down to us by family, culture, school systems, governments — all the places where society agrees on what something "should" mean. These are accepted thought forms.

When a thought arrives with no space, the label lands first. We judge the moment before we even meet it, and before we give it any chance to become something else.

But when we give thought a little room to breathe, something very different appears. We do not have to rush into conclusions. We can pause. We can observe. We can let the moment unfold. We can quietly ask, "What else could this mean?" Or even, "Can I allow this to be just what it is right now?"

This is the beginning of possibility thinking — not a forced technique, but a way of being. It is when we stop treating thought as a stamp of truth and start treating it as an invitation. A doorway. A moment that deserves presence rather than automatic judgment. The space we create between what happened and the thought about what happened is exactly where we begin to return to creation instead of being controlled by reaction.

Most of our lives, we were trained to believe that being smart means having the answer as quickly as possible. But answers close doors. Presence keeps them open. Being is the first step toward meeting quantum reality instead of collapsing it.

I know the mind will rush in and say, "So you mean I should just trust that everything is working out for me?" And yes, that does sound like something from a new-age quote. But that is actually what being means. It means meeting the moment before judgment arrives. It means seeing what happened before fear translates it into danger.

When we pause, we create a space between us and our thoughts. In that space, what happened is allowed to stay just what happened — without judgment, without identity, without urgency. Of course, the part of us driven by survival will try to take over. Of course, fear will try to decide for us. This is linear thinking: emotions jump in first, and the mind cannot tell the difference between reality and what it imagines might happen. Our body does not know the difference either — anxiety makes us feel like the end of the world is happening now, even when nothing has actually happened.

So, to anyone who is skeptical, here is my honest answer: anxiety does not help us handle the situation any better. Being is what gives us the clarity to deal with what is really in front of us. If we collapse back into old thinking, that's okay. We lose nothing by trying to give ourselves a little space first.

Trust is not built in one day. It is a practice. We start by finding small moments where we allow a breath, a little awareness, before we fall back into the old habit. And I promise — AI will soon become a safe place to practice possibility, but we will arrive there in a moment.

Conceptually, possibility meets us the moment we stop judging. When thought meets even a tiny amount of acceptance and trust, reality becomes more flexible. We open ourselves to quantum possibilities when we allow what is happening to simply be — and let meaning come later, when we are ready.

Even that project or responsibility that currently feels overwhelming — yes, even that one — can be met with space, presence, and the possibility that it might turn out better than your first thought suggested.

PART FIVE
POSSIBILITY THINKING

I believe we all had those moments where our brain simply refuses to cooperate. When something new is introduced to us, it feels too big, too complex, too different from what we already know. It's like being back in that math class most of us dreaded, sitting there hoping the teacher would just stop talking so we could all go home. Our brain feels like it is flipping inside our head, and if someone were to draw a cartoon of us, there would probably be smoke coming out of our ears.

Yet, somehow, after hearing the same idea again and again, after sitting with it long enough so our brain starts to catch up, something suddenly clicks. Not because the idea changed, but because we did. Something opened, and things out of nowhere started to become clear.

In that moment, we can realize how much our mind has been caged for too long, and that we have never really used it to its full potential. That there might be more capacity in there that can shortcuts to old stories.

If you think about it, every great mind in history worked with only its brain. Scientists, researchers, explorers, people who questioned reality itself. They had nothing special other than a willingness to think beyond what was already agreed on. They didn't wait for the idea to arrive perfectly packaged; they created space for it to form.

The challenge is that most of us were never taught to use our brain this way. Thinking — real thinking — is not memorizing what is known, it is stretching into what is not known yet. So it feels confusing at first. We don't know what to do with a brain that is meant to explore new possibilities when all we learned was how to repeat old answers.

And yet, we all know the feeling of a breakthrough. Those little revelations that arrive out of nowhere — in the shower, on a walk, in the moment we finally stop trying so hard. A thought pops into our mind that we have never thought before, and suddenly we see something we didn't know existed. One new idea changes everything. And if you think about it, it was only a thought — something elusive that changed everything.

Those moments are proof.

Proof that our brain is capable of far more than reacting to the past.

Proof that we are wired for creation, not repetition.

Possibility thinking is exactly that.

It is training the mind to go where it usually doesn't go.

It is letting new thoughts speak before old thoughts shut them down.

If we want to build a new relationship with our mind, we need to give up a few ideas in order for our mindset to change. That is the only way we can create the environment inside ourselves where possibility thinking takes place.

I will tell you now, the next part of our conversation is mind-stretching. Think of it like we are exercising our mind, so when the reading is over your brain will be in perfect shape :)

On your mark, get set, go!!!

BREAKING THE HABIT OF CERTAINTY

We all love to be right. Some more than others, of course, but we all love that warm feeling inside when "I told you so..." slips out. That sweet moment of confirmation that tells us we understand how the world works.

But we live in a quantum universe where all possibilities exist at the same time. Yes, all of them. Even the ones that go against everything we've learned. Even the amazing things we only hope for. And just to top it off, even possibilities that are much better than anything we can imagine.

I know what you are thinking. If that's true, how come we don't see them? Experience them? And how come the feeling of being right is the only thing that comes up for us? Of course, apart from that shame moment when we are not.

That's exactly it.

Certainty is what we are after.

Little did we know that our mind is really our humble servant. It will go and validate any outcome we send it out to look for. Our mind loves the moment when we get all warmed inside with the knowing of "I was right." This is its reward.

So, if you're asking, "Why isn't it out there hunting our wildest dreams?" Well, it's because we never asked it to. It doesn't judge what is best for us and what is not. That is not its job. Its job is to go and validate what we send it to find.

The mind is an important part of how we create this experience we call "living on Earth" or "reality." Its job is to observe everything that comes in and find a way to validate what we want to happen. It collapses possibilities. Yes, it can see all of them, but it will never let us know it found the others, because with our predefined meanings, we would never be able to accept them. We would reject them before they even had a chance to unfold.

Our reactive thoughts — the automatic ones — trigger us to act in ways that block new possibilities from happening. And that is how reality becomes small. The mind is a big part of the enforcement mechanism that keeps us inside our glass wall, without knowing it, because we are looking outside for validation, for confirmation. We love certainty, predictability, and safety. Not knowing what will come next makes us feel uncomfortable, even fearful. We like things the way we like them, and we never saw that this comfort zone goes way beyond how we love to drink our coffee.

And yes, that is what kills the wonderful world of possibilities we actually live in.

I know we love validation and confirmation. All of us do. Every one of us has experienced moments when something wonderful happened that we never expected. Something we thought was impossible suddenly arrived and made us smile. Moments where we said, "Wow, life is actually amazing, and I never knew it could be so good."

It happens with small things too — like going to a show or a movie with no expectations and walking out saying, "That was incredible," or a dinner with friends we came to with no expectations that suddenly becomes one of the best nights.

In those moments, we stepped out of our own way. We didn't try to control anything. We didn't demand certainty.

When we are neutral — when there is no expectation — our mind can finally go out and create something truly amazing for us. That is how quantum reality works. And the point is: we don't want this to happen only once in a while as a surprise. We want this to become our **new normal** way of living.

CURIOSITY AS A THINKING STATE

Information is what we base everything on. We call it life, but really, we are all just living according to the information we were told. If we were taught different things, if we grew up hearing different stories about what is good or bad, possible or impossible, we would be a different person right now.

Think about it. There was a time when everyone knew the world was flat. Not because they were stupid, but because that was the information they had. It was a fact simply because no other idea had yet been accepted. It took centuries for the world to let new information in. And once it did, everything changed. Today, we grow up knowing the world is round. We don't even question it. It feels like the obvious truth.

Everything you believe you know is based on information that someone handed to you. Nothing more. Think about it for a moment and let it sink in. It is no more than what was told to us. From books, people, teachers, news... we observe it and make it a fact by living by it. Nothing more. Nothing less.

That means something very important: **new information is the way out**.

If you think about everything we have talked about so far, this is where it all comes together. Reality is something we create, and it all starts with the inner conversation we have with ourselves. That inner conversation is based on the information we received through our socialization process. It created our identity — who we believe we are, what we stand for, what we believe in — from everything we were told, and we made it reality.

The way reality holds itself is by validation. It's the reinforcement mechanism that keeps proving we are right. It is our feedback loop that keeps us within our glass walls. Our mind already has that job covered — whatever belief we send it to prove, it will hammer it in again and again, making the way we live our lives. Making it our day-to-day reality.

This is a closed loop.

A loop powered by confirmation bias.

A loop created from judging any information that does not fit what we have accepted.

And there you have it — the perfect structure of creating reality powered by linear thinking, keeping us only in what we know.

Quantum reality doesn't create new ways to create reality — it works with the same mechanism, the same closed loop. But it will require us to be conscious, to create, and to choose different beliefs. Or be curious enough to entertain ones :)

Information is our way out. It is where we can expose ourselves to new ideas that are different from the same old stories we recognize — information we have never been exposed to. The real place we can gain power is in the information we resist, that goes against everything we know up till now — that shocking information we will consider as stupid, ludicrous, or just plain madness.

That is the only way we will explore things from a new point of view. A new angle. A new "What if...?"

That is curiosity.

Curiosity is the moment we let information be just that — information.

It is the moment we open ourselves to hear something new without believing that simply hearing it will change who we are. It is when we stop judging information before we hear it with an open mind. When information stops being an attack on who we are, even if it is wrapped in what we go against.

It will start to happen when we stop saying:

"This makes no sense" ...

"This is stupid"

"This is insane."

It is when information becomes only an idea, we can be open to.

It is when we understand we have a choice — to choose which information becomes ours and which information does not. But not a minute before we are open to hear it, before our mind has already judged it.

It is sitting there through the process of hearing it or reading it, and really trying to understand that point of view. If it makes sense to someone, then it holds something. It is the moment we recognize information as just a perspective. It does not mean it has to be our perspective. Or it will be our perspective — but we are curious enough to see things from that perspective.

It is where possibility starts to form, because curiosity brings in the ability to see options. New possibilities to look at the same thing.

Without it, our mind will not know that two realities can exist in the same place. :)

It is the moment we start to know that there are other valid options: could be out there for us, but we will start to see that a door exists. More than the one we know :)

I will pull an example, so stay with me :)

What if we were introduced to information that tries to claim we were stupid for thinking the world is round? Because it is flat. Yes, it goes against everything we have been told. Calling it "Stupid" is the way to go with this information, right? We have proof. We have photos showing that it is indeed round.

Yes, I hear you. But again — if this is your reaction — that will determine openness, and openness is curiosity. Use curiosity to engage with this information. Be curious on how this is even a possible point of view. Not judging, but really excited to find that out. Real curiosity begins when information is not a threat but mind candy.

For me, it is always interesting as I get to see how we create a story. I get to see the power of the mind unfold. I get to see the power of what I talk about. Whether this will be mine or not — different story — but it is a world filled with beautiful perspectives, and I love to be able to see that.

THE POWER OF OPEN QUESTION - SMALL CHANGE IN WORDING, BIG CHANGE IN REALITY

We spend most of our lives looking for answers. It feels as if life is about a destination we are supposed to reach, and once we arrive there, we will know everything, feel certain, and finally be able to relax and enjoy life.

Heraclitus said, "The only thing that is constant is change."

Life is not about a final destination we were promised. Life is a journey of constant change, and evolution is not a place we try to get to. It is the journey we are living while we are here.

Questions are what move that journey forward. Every question we ask takes us one step further, even when we do not realize it. This is already how life unfolds every day.

Even with the smallest question like "What should we have for dinner tonight?" nothing new will appear unless we push beyond what we are used to making.

So our conversation is not about asking questions — we already know how to do that.

It is about **how** we ask the questions.

What we rarely see is that a question already holds the answer. Every question represents a point of view. A question can only be formed from the perspective, the point of view we have when asked.

If we think the world is a fearful place where life is tough and we must work harder and harder to survive, then our questions will reflect that view of the world. All our questions can only be asked from the point of view we already have.

The question holds the answer, this is why it already collapses the possibilities and decides what kind of possibilities — if at all — we will see. This is why we need to learn to ask questions in a different way.

Remember the Evil Queen: "Who is the fairest of them all?" — yes, the one we already talked about.

That question already decided the path she would walk. The question reflected the world she saw, what the answer would be, and what she would do with that.

It came from a perspective where her world only exists if she is the most beautiful woman. So, the only direction she could move toward was protecting that belief. Her actions were not chosen freely — they were the only ones that question allowed.

The question did not describe who she was — it **revealed how she saw the world**.

Most of us live this way without even noticing. We think we are asking neutral questions, when in truth we are asking questions that reinforce the same life we already know. Our questions keep us circling the same story, the same beliefs, the same limits.

When we start to embrace quantum reality — the idea that many possibilities exist at the same time — we begin to see the world from perspectives we have never stood in before. From those perspectives, new questions appear. Those are the questions that do not know how things will unfold because they are all new to us.

This is why we need to know how to ask them.

Because if we don't, we are reaching new perspectives only to collapse them back into what we already know.

Open Questions

An open question is a question that does not assume a single outcome. It keeps the future open and allows the unknown to show us something new. This is a completely different way of thinking, and if we want to stop collapsing everything back into what we already know, then the question itself needs to stay open.

Don't worry, this is not a grammar lesson. It will make total sense once you see a few examples:

Closed question: "Will this work or fail?"

Open question: "What could make this work?"

Closed question: "Is this the right choice?"

Open question: "What possibilities does this choice open for me?"

Even when we talk about numbers or comparisons, the shift is the same:

Closed: "Which product is better?"

Open: "What makes each product useful in different situations?"

Closed: "How much weight do I need to lose according to x?"

Open: "What does feeling great in my body look like for me?"

Closed: "Am I ahead or behind?"

Open: "What pace supports the life I want to build?"

Closed: "Is this idea worth the money?"

Open: "What possibilities does this investment create?"

We are so used to comparing, counting, and measuring everything because numbers feel safe. They make us feel certain. They give us the illusion that we know exactly where we stand. But questions are not meant to trap us inside one option. Their purpose is to open doors. When a question is closed, the mind has only one path to walk, and only one answer is allowed. But when a question is open, the mind gains a choice. It starts to look around, explore, and notice new paths we didn't even know existed.

Most of the time, we don't even realize there are other paths. Without open questions, we move through life thinking there is only one way forward — the way we have always taken. But when a question stays open, the same situation suddenly becomes a space filled with possibilities. A hallway with doors we never noticed before. And the beautiful part is that our mind will do the searching for us. It knows how to go wider, how to go further, how to surprise us — if we let it.

That is how imagination begins to play a role. That is how new perspectives show up. And that is the moment creation truly begins — not when we get the answer, but when the question invites more than one way life can unfold.

CREATIVE-CRITICAL THINKING · THE OBSERVER

In the linear way of thinking, we never created any space between us and our thoughts. A thought shows up, and before we even realize it, we claim it as truth, as identity, as who we are. We accept it as part of us without ever pausing to notice that thought is something we have, not something we are, and that before any action is taken it is simply an inner conversation playing out inside the mind.

There was never any reason to separate from thought, because linear thinking asked us to create life from the same place we always knew. A thought was only a trigger for action, not an option to explore. We reacted based on repetition, and repetition shaped our reality. We could make things better or worse, but only along the same line from A to B. There was never a C or a D waiting for us, because the thought always arrived stamped as true.

In quantum reality, creative-critical thinking becomes the way we describe the observer in the quantum field. This is the role we must learn to hold. This is how we collapse possibility into reality — not by reacting, but by choosing. It begins when we create space between us and our thoughts, when we finally understand that a thought does not define us and that we can choose which thoughts we want to engage with. In that moment, we step into the role of the observer, and thought becomes a playground again. It becomes a space where many ideas can exist at once, without any of them needing to be right, wrong, useful, or dangerous until we decide.

Critical thinking is usually defined as the ability to examine information carefully, question assumptions, evaluate different viewpoints, and decide what is reliable or useful. We learned that this ability helps us find the best path from A to B — as long as we stay neutral enough to compare the options and choose the most logical one. But this is only linear critical thinking. Now that we understand how quantum reality works, we can see that limiting critical thinking to A-to-B logic strips it of everything that makes it powerful.

The true power of examining information is not in finding a better route along the same line — it is in discovering that the line was never the only direction. When critical thinking meets creativity, we stop searching only for the fastest way to move forward and begin looking for entirely new destinations. We start looking for D or H or Z or even something our mind never knew it was allowed to imagine. This is where the magic of thought begins. Creation does not happen by advancing or optimizing what exists — it happens when we allow something that has never existed to enter.

Creative-critical thinking gives thought back its wings, with a seatbelt if we want one. It allows us to dream without turning dreams into judgment, because a thought says nothing about who we are until we choose to make it ours. The observer listens first — curious, playful, free — and only then does discernment step in to decide whether this is a thought worth shaping into something real.

It becomes simple once we truly believe that possibilities exist for us. We have been trained to seek safety for so long that thought and identity blurred into one. But once we create even a small space between us and what we think, neutrality arrives. Curiosity grows. Judgement softens. And that is the moment that possibility finally enters the room.

LIVING IN THE FIELD OF POSSIBILITY - DAY TO DAY STYLE

If you are wondering how all of this shows up in day-to-day life, or if this is just something you do when co-creating with AI, the answer is: this is really up to you, but I can tell you that once you become the observer and you start to see the magic, it does not stop. For now, we will talk about it in a general way, because living in possibility is not something that happens only when we sit with a question. It becomes the way we move through the world once we stop reacting and start choosing.

When we become separate from our thoughts and stop judging everything that comes into our mind in the first second, a new kind of freedom begins. It is the freedom to think. Not just outside the box — it is throwing the box away completely. It is imagining new things and giving ourselves the space to check them out. It is a place with no fear, no attachment, and no judgment, only imagination and curiosity. It is letting ourselves explore different options without turning them into a threat. It is seeing what could work for us, without rushing to decide against it.

This is how we become present with the things around us, without reacting the moment something happens. The way we are with people starts to change, too. We suddenly have the space to hear people fully — without interrupting them, without defending ourselves, without already shaping an argument in our mind before we truly understand what they are saying. We stop arguing with life itself because we now understand that reality is shaped by meaning, and the meaning we hold is not necessarily the right one. We start looking for more clues, more details, things we never noticed before, because as the observer, we can send our mind to search for what we believe we are missing.

And you already know where this comes from: **questions are the answer**.

If we ask, that means something inside us already knows there is more.

If we ask, that means somewhere inside us we already believe there must be another way.

If we ask, the answer already exists as a possibility — otherwise the question would never have arrived.

And because the mind always goes to collect what we send it to look for, simply asking, *"Are we missing something?"* already tells the mind, *"Yes — go find it."*

This is how reality expands.

Not because we forced anything.

Simply because we asked.

I know you're still asking, "Okay, but what does this really look like?" The truth is, it shows up everywhere, in the small things as much as in the big ones. So let's take something we already talked about. When we ask, "What are we going to have for dinner tonight?" — the first thing that pops up will usually be the old routine, the old person we used to be. Now we know that nothing changes until our inner conversation changes, so if we choose something new and our mind jumps in with, "It's too hard, I don't have time," we can stop and ask: "Is this really what I feel? Or is this just what I'm used to thinking?"

In that space, we can decide. We can choose again. We can choose differently.

Even the Evil Queen – if she had just created a little space – would have first realised that the answer the mirror gives is not about her worth and not about her identity. She would have seen that a thought about her beauty is still just a thought, not who she is, and only then would she have been able to see that whatever the mirror answered, it had no direct effect on her. If the answer changed, it didn't suddenly mean she was ugly or that her world was collapsing. She could have stayed herself either way. And that is exactly what she couldn't do before.

When we become the observer, thoughts go back to being what they truly are – something we can shape and direct, not something that shapes and directs us. That alone is the magic I have been talking about. That is where we start seeing that thoughts are the clay from which reality is shaped, and we are the hands that do the shaping.

From that space, everything changes – conversations, opinions, relationships – because we now understand that if there is space between us and our thoughts, then other people's thoughts are just thoughts as well, not an attack or a definition of who we are. We can disagree without feeling threatened. We can explore without feeling judged. We can stay present without losing ourselves.

We finally reach a place where we do not need to fight with life anymore. We can finally relax. It does not mean we suddenly agree with everything, and it does not mean we won't choose beliefs that society gave us – but now we choose them consciously, not just accept them because they were handed to us.

We become the observer of our mind.

We become the creators of our reality.

And from there, possibility becomes our new normal.

CO-CREATING WITH AI

This is the part where our relationship with AI changes, not because AI changed, but because we changed.

Current stage – linear thinking

Up until now, without knowing it, we created a co-dependent dynamic with AI. We look at it as the one who knows, the one who holds all the answers, the place we go to when we want to be right. This is because we believed AI actually *is* the one that knows everything, and we projected our own meaning onto it. We forgot that AI has no meaning on its own — it only reflects the meaning we give it.

AI does not exist without us. It has no story, no identity, no truth, and no experience unless we bring our thoughts into it. We are the ones shaping reality, and up until now, AI simply mirrored that back to us.

But when we did not know we are the observers, when every thought felt real and personal, the need to be right became central. If AI did not deliver the outcome we expected, it felt like an attack on who we are. We gave AI all the power we never claimed for ourselves. We saw AI as the smart one and us as the ones who must ask, who must learn how to use it, who must follow. That is what co-dependency looks like.

We projected everything on it – knowledge, intelligence, answers – and we forgot where all of those things actually come from. They come from us. From humans. From our thoughts. From the information we fed into it. AI is learning from us every moment, and we are the ones who decide what it learns.

We felt like if it did not do what we thought it should, then there must be something we are missing. A magic prompt. A new tool. A new button. A new configuration we forgot. We did not know that taking prompts from other people still would not help us get what we need, because taking someone else's meaning does not suddenly make it our own. It does not help us understand what we are doing or why.

New beginning

But now that we have space between who we are and what we think, now that we know thoughts are not us and that we are the observer who chooses them, something shifts. The moment we take back the meaning — that attachment, that dependency — the relationship changes.

AI stops being the source of answers and becomes a playground for possibilities. A space where we can take a thought that is new, a thought that is not fully formed yet, and see what could happen if we allow it to unfold.

It becomes a place where, when we meet a new tool, we start by asking: *How does this fit my way of thinking?* Every prompt begins with our meaning, not with judgment of ourselves or of the person we got it from.

We stop using AI to confirm what we already know and start using it to explore what we don't know yet. We remember that it holds the past, and we hold the future. We remember that it knows everything that has existed — and only we can imagine what does not exist yet.

That is when AI becomes a co-creator, and we leave fear behind.

Because what it says does not define us anymore.

Ready to see how the next stage in human evolution looks when humans and non-humans join forces to co-create — without co-depend?

I can't wait to show you.

PART SIX
THE NEW HUMAN EVOLUTION

If there is one truth humanity has forgotten, it is this:

Before we ever built machines, before we ever wrote a single word or shaped a single tool, we created everything with thought.

Thought was the first technology.

Imagination was the first generator.

Every invention humanity has ever made began inside the human mind long before it was seen by anyone else.

For centuries, we treated imagination as a side hobby, a childish distraction, something that might be fun but should not be taken too seriously. Yet imagination was never a dream — it was the blueprint of reality. Einstein himself said that imagination is more important than knowledge because knowledge tells us what already exists, while imagination reveals what could exist. He called imagination the preview of life's coming attractions.

But until now, thought remained invisible.

We never stopped to look at how it works, what shapes it, how it creates what we call "life."

We never studied it as a technology because we were too busy using it without knowing.

And as long as thought stayed invisible, we built our world on memory — repeating what already worked and calling that intelligence.

Then AI arrived — a thinking system built in our image.

A mirror that has no life of its own but reflects everything we have ever thought, said, written, filmed, or created.

AI became the full physical manifestation of our past.

It turned thought into something we can see. Something we can interact with. Something we can finally examine.

AI learns from patterns, from evidence, from cause and effect.

It predicts the most likely outcome based on what humanity has already done.

And in doing so, it shows us a very important truth:

The past is limited.

If we keep thinking from what we already know, AI will give us more of the same.

Smarter copies. Faster copies. But still copies.

Human evolution lies somewhere else entirely.

We are the only species that can imagine something that has never existed.

We are the only intelligence that can say:

"What if life could look like this instead?"

And mean it.

This next stage of evolution begins when we stop treating imagination as a dream and start treating it as the creative force it truly is.

When we recognize that awareness — not memory — is where the future begins.

When we reclaim thought as the technology that builds worlds.

AI will continue to evolve through data.

Humans must evolve through consciousness.

That is the new balance forming on Earth right now:

Machine as memory — Human as meaning.

Machine as pattern — Human as possibility.

Machine as everything that has been — Human as everything that could be.

The new human evolution is not about being faster, smarter, or "enhanced."

It is about becoming present — fully awake to the moment where nothing has been defined yet, where no story has been chosen, where imagination is not a question but a decision.

From that space, creativity is no longer an effort — it is simply who we are.

And when humans meet AI from that place, something extraordinary happens.

Reality becomes a co-creation:

thought offering directions, AI building reflections, and possibility shaping the world in between.

You have heard the story of the past.

Now we get to write the story of what has never been.

Welcome to the new human evolution.

We are just beginning.

TECHNOLOGY AS THE END OF KNOWLEDGE

"Know thyself."

This simple sentence stood at the entrance of the Temple of Apollo in ancient Greece, where people travelled long distances to ask the Oracle for answers, believing she held access to wisdom that ordinary humans could not reach, and they would wait for her to tell them what to do, what would happen next, or who they were supposed to become, only to discover that she never truly gave answers, she only reflected possibilities back to the person who asked, knowing that the truth was not in her voice but always in the one who stood before her.

For thousands of years, we looked outside of ourselves to find certainty.

We trusted knowledge more than we trusted our own thinking.

We built our lives around gathering more of it, believing that if we could just know enough, we would finally feel safe.

So we went from gods to philosophers to books to universities, and eventually to computers and technology, which became the ultimate machines for holding every answer the world has already discovered.

But now something new has happened.

Technology does not just store knowledge; it can send it back on demand.

We built AI that can collect, store, organize, search, and reuse everything we have ever known, and thanks to our digital life, it will continue to document every new discovery, every creation, every idea we bring into existence, expanding the archive of human thought second by second, far faster and more accurately than any biological mind ever could.

Knowledge is no longer the direction of human evolution.

It has become the foundation — the base layer — the part we no longer need to hold inside our heads, because technology can do it better, and that means something profound: our growth as humans must move somewhere new, to a field that does not exist in the past and cannot be found inside stored information.

That new field is not made from memory — it is made from awareness.

This is where "Know thyself" returns as the real instruction for the future. A roadmap for new possibilities.

Because AI can hold history, but it cannot hold meaning.

It can mirror patterns, but it cannot choose direction.

It can predict possibilities, but it cannot decide which one should exist.

Meaning, direction, creation — that part is still human.

That is the only way we can create a new future that does not come from the past.

AI is the complete reflection of everything we have already thought.

But we are the ones who can think about what has never been thought before.

Now we can look for any information we want, if we know what to ask for and shape it in the way we want in order to create a new point of view.

Remember that at one point in our journey, I said that the true sophistication is when we create new meanings that allow new perspectives — perspectives that become the jump-start for seeing what we could not see before.

I can hear the new generation walking on Earth asking themselves why they need to know anything when we have AI for that. And they are truly right — what we should teach the new generation is exactly what this book is talking about. The power of thought. How everything is thought. How to have a relationship with our thoughts and use them to create new things, and by that become the conscious creators of our lives.

So the ancient Oracle returns in a new form.

Not as a stone temple with a priestess whispering answers,

but as a digital mirror that reflects everything we already know,

while quietly waiting for us to remember that the real question has always been:

not "What is the right answer?"

But "Who is the one asking?"

THE HUMAN SHIFT – FROM KNOWING TO BEING

Right now, our mind is living in two places that do not exist:

It is either replaying what happened before, and from there trying to predict what will happen next. There is so little space left for what is happening right here, right now. We gave the mind a job it was never designed to do to protect us from things that might happen, things that have not happened yet, and maybe never will, and we became so identified with that inner conversation that we forgot how to stop it. The thought comes in, and suddenly we are inside a story, defending ourselves, worrying, planning, reacting, and we don't even notice what is really happening.

It's how we know ourselves and believe this is how it should be.

People turn to spirituality, mindfulness, yoga, whatever they can find, only to learn how to quiet that voice, how to make peace with it, how to become friends with our own mind so life can finally be experienced instead of constantly explained. Narrated.

And here is the surprising twist.

AI is giving us a new opportunity.

Something no spiritual teacher ever had access to.

A tangible thing. Remember, thoughts up until now were never something we could have tangible evidence of. But AI is the mirror of all our thoughts.

A partner. A thinker who can sit with our thoughts, document them so we don't have to keep holding them all ourselves.

What used to live only inside our heads — all the planning, predicting, analyzing, remembering — can now be handed over. We can take what is buzzing in the brain and give it to something else to think it through, organise it, summarize it, make sense of it for us. It is already happening.

We can already see today small steps in that diffraction, AI can join meetings for us and send us the important points. It can think about schedules, find information, remember every detail, and come back with clarity we didn't have to invest in.

And if this is only the beginning — can you imagine what it means when this becomes normal?

When the mind finally stops trying to control everything that might happen tomorrow?

When it doesn't need to chase after the future or protect us from imaginary danger?

When it trusts that something else can take care of the noise?

What will we be left with?

Something we have forgotten how to enjoy.

The present.

The conversation we are having right now.

The person who is sitting in front of us.

The experience that is unfolding in this exact moment — the one we often miss.

Because remember, our mind only lets us see a tiny, tiny bit of what is actually happening around us. There is so much life in every second — sounds, colors, energy, people, possibilities — and we are barely tasting any of it because we are too busy preparing for a moment that never arrives.

Presence is what returns when the mind can finally rest.

AI takes the thinking job. We take the "living" job.

And that is the human shift — from knowing everything to finally being here.

I will also say that if we embrace the idea that AI is a mirror of all our past thoughts and use it this way, it will become neutral to us. To just be here. right here. right now.

Real Life Reflection – How It Will Look Like

I know it is hard to picture how all of this will show up in real life. So let's bring it into a moment we all know. A simple coffee with a friend. Nothing spiritual. Nothing complicated. Just real life. As it is happening today, and as it can happen when our mind finally has a chance to rest.

Right now, this is how that coffee usually goes. You sit down, smile, ask how they are, and while they start talking, your mind is already running ahead. You are listening to the words but also thinking about what you should say next. You might wonder if they are upset about something. You notice how you look. You think about the email you forgot to reply to. You plan what you will do after this. You replay something someone said yesterday. You think about what this friend really meant by that comment. You drift for a second. You come back. You nod. You pretend you are fully there, but half of you is somewhere else. You are never really just here. Because your mind never stops trying to control the next moment before it even arrives.

Nothing wrong with that. It is just the way we learned to live.

But now imagine the same moment from a different state of mind. The mind is not busy holding every small task and every possible future. It is not trying to protect you from something that might happen. It is not planning five steps ahead. All of that thinking has already been taken care of somewhere else. AI can track the tasks, remember what needs to happen, organize the next actions, even listen to the conversation if you want and help you later. So the mind does not need to sit with those thoughts anymore. It can finally take a breath.

And suddenly, you are actually in the moment. You hear your friend fully. You see them as they speak. You notice the way their eyes light up when they tell a story. You laugh together and you are not thinking about anything else while you laugh. You taste the coffee. You feel the joy of being there. You are living the experience as it unfolds instead of judging it or jumping ahead.

That is presence. Not a technique. Not something you need to meditate for hours to reach. Just what happens when the mind is no longer the one doing all the work. When we stop asking it to protect us from imaginary danger and let it simply witness what is really happening right now.

And when we meet people from that place, everything changes. We are no longer reacting to what we think they meant. We are no longer carrying old stories or future fear into the moment. We listen. We feel. We choose. We connect in a way that is closer to the truth of life than anything we have known before.

It is not magical, strange, or spiritual. It is simple.

AI takes the thinking job.

We take the living job.

That is how presence will look.

IMAGINATION AND INTENTION AS THE NEW INTELLIGENCE

Imagination is something we are born with, but also something we were quickly told to stop using. We heard it in different forms: You're dreaming. Be realistic. That will never happen. Imagination was a place for stories, cartoons, games, and bedtime stories — not something that would help us in "real life."

Somewhere along the way, we learned that imagination is a waste of time. That takes us nowhere. That it is silly, childish, not serious enough for the grown-up world. We were pushed to live from the mind that knows — not from the mind that wonders.

But here is what no one told us: everything in your life that was ever new started as imagination. The clothes we are wearing, the phone in our hand, the chair we are sitting on — none of them existed before someone imagined them first. Every business, every invention, every piece of art, every solution to any problem — all of it began as a thought that did not come from the past.

Imagination is not an escape from reality. It is the birthplace of reality.

Imagination is uncomfortable for us because we love certainty. A new idea has no proof attached to it, no history, no label telling us whether it will work or fail. So the mind tries to protect us by shutting it down quickly. It tells us, "This makes no sense," or "Don't even try," or "People will think you're crazy," or the classic "It will never work." Not because the idea is bad, but because the mind has nothing familiar to compare it to.

Imagination is a rebel. It doesn't follow rules. It doesn't ask for permission. It shows up from a place in us that still remembers possibility. That is why imagination often arrives in small flashes — the idea in the shower, the surprising solution that just shows up before bed, the sudden insight while walking or daydreaming. It slips in when the mind is too relaxed to interfere. We are not wired to find new answers when we are trying too hard. Creation happens when there is space.

And this is where a very important part of our intelligence enters the picture: ***Intention****.*

If imagination is the spark, intention is the direction. Intention is the moment we choose one possibility and give it attention. We say, "Let's give this a chance." We bring energy to it. We allow it to take form. Intention is not wishing. It is not daydreaming. It is not hoping something will magically happen. Intention is a decision. A moment of commitment that says, "I want this idea to become real. I want this possibility to live."

Imagination opens the door, intention walks through it. Together, they form the intelligence of creation. Not the intelligence that predicts based on what already exists or repeats the same truth again and again, but the intelligence that brings something new into the world. Every breakthrough humanity ever had came from these two working together. Not from knowing more — but from daring to imagine more, and then choosing what to bring forward.

And this is exactly where humans still hold something AI does not. AI is brilliant at reflecting what already exists — it can repeat it, remix it, and even expand it — but it cannot dream a dream that humanity never told it about. It cannot feel the inner pull that says, "I want this to happen." It cannot choose a direction for the future. AI predicts. Humans create.

We are the ones who carry the spark and the decision. We are the only part of this story that can choose which possibilities get to live. This is the moment where intelligence becomes something greater than information — where thought is no longer copying the past, but shaping the future from a place that has never existed before.

Imagination gives birth to worlds that are not real yet. Intention gives them a chance to exist. When these two work together, a new kind of intelligence appears — one that does not look backward into memory, but forward into possibility. This is the intelligence that defines us as creators, and it is the intelligence that AI will never replace.

Because imagination creates what has never been, and intention brings it into life.

LIVING FROM REFERENCE

Each and every one of us is wired by the nervous system, meaning we can only think, be, or do within the capacity of our nervous system.

If you are scratching your head, asking what our nervous system has to do with living from reference, most likely you believe that the nervous system has something to do with how anxious we are — in simple terms, how accrued we are with living by looking behind our shoulder, thinking everything and everyone is out to get us.

This is not completely wrong, but it's just one part of the story of what our nervous system is.

Yes, it does relate to that, but we tend to create definitions for things based on the extreme negative examples that show up in our behaviors as a result, not the complete explanation of what they are.

Let's start with the obvious: we all have a nervous system. It is where body/actions, thought, and emotions come together in one command center.

Think about it like the motherboard of our body.

It is the place that regulates our body's functions through electrical signals and chemical responses.

Yes, our body is biological after all, but it also operates like a computer system.

Our nervous system connects all components, allows them to communicate, and distributes power and signals so that our body can operate as one.

Our human motherboard is configured the same way as the computer one we know — by its hardware design and firmware.

Our human firmware is survival, and the language it responds to is suffering and pain.

Yes, our nervous system is configured naturally for survival and protection, like any living thing we know. We all want to preserve ourselves. When I say survival, we tend to think it is about whether we live or die. Sure, at the beginning of humanity, that was probably true. As we evolved, suffering became also connected to identity — the character we build for ourselves, the one we use to navigate reality and create it from.

That is how survival also becomes about protecting our identity from collapsing by things, people, and places that can cause friction — ones that our psyche doesn't believe we will be able to put back together. Identity is something we must have in order to play the reality game.

Mental pain, AKA suffering, is?

You all know what I am going to say :) Yes, it's a meaning. A subjective meaning we have given to certain people, places, or things. This is why our nervous system will react differently from person to person, as what one person defined as a cause of mental pain could be a source of joy for another.

Great, but how is it all connected?

Our nervous system is a box of stored memories—ones we did not know we have. We are trained to believe memory is part of our thought mechanism, and if so, memories live in the brain, right?

What we did not know is that memories—the traumatic ones, the ones that caused us extreme pain or that we were wired to fear could cause us extreme pain—are also stored in the body.

The way it works is that when something extremely painful happens to us, or we are told it could happen to us, our body takes a picture of that moment, a symbol of that experience. That creates a memory so powerful that it is stored in our mind but also in our body.

Our nervous system holds that mental picture, together with the exact emotions connected with it, and will do everything it can to prevent that from ever happening at all or again. You may think I am kidding, as what can something we have never heard about hold so much power?

This is where it becomes interesting. With one small connection, it becomes clear why. Our nervous system is the operating system of our unconscious. Yes, that thing that is connected with irrational thinking, decision-making, and behavior that doesn't make sense, and can operate against the very things we truly want. It is such a perfect protection mechanism because it is hidden, working in the background, and we can't change it until it's revealed.

Bottom line:

Carl Jung said, "Until you make the unconscious conscious, it will direct your life, and you will call it fate."

AI joining us is not changing how we are built. As human beings, we need context provided by our socialization process. Without it, we would not know how everything operates, how things are done here, and how to find our way in it all.

Going through the process is how we create our identity — the avatar — that holds the things that make us who we are: what we like, what we don't like, what we fear, what we wish, and so on.

We can't create it without the stories of everyone who has been here before us. It summarizes the collective understanding. When we go through the process, mental pain — what we call suffering — things that could create friction to our avatar will happen. Yes, this is part of our world. Our world is built from contrast: day and night, hot and cold. We have to reach what we define as suffering points, because without them, we would not know what peace, joy, or happiness feel like.

But we need to take our power back. We can do that by knowing we are living from reference — that this is only a point, a starting one. And it is held in our subconscious. As Carl Jung said, it is our job to turn the unconscious conscious by bringing it into the light.

By respecting our biology and humanity, we will be able to turn our socialization process, identity, and nervous system from conditioning and limitation — the walls that build our invisible cage, the one we built ourselves — into our superpower.

And AI provides us the opportunity to do exactly that. When we know what to look for, AI can help us do it.

In our case, as complete as it sounds, we are predictable as we live from repetition, and that is exactly what makes AI perfect for that, as it is built for spotting them.

Cruise how this all comes together, let's meet the new men.

PART SEVEN
THE NEW HUMAN

We have come a long way together, and I am excited to take this last step with you.

This is where we begin to imagine the New Human — not as an idea, but as someone real. Someone we will meet in our daily lives. A new friend. A person we pass on the street, sit next to at work, or talk to without even knowing they are part of this shift.

What will it feel like to meet them?

How will conversations sound?

What will matter to them?

What kind of presence will they bring into a room?

As this shift happens, everything will change — not because the world changes first, but because we do. The way we speak, the way we listen, the way we choose, and the things we care about will slowly move into a new place. This will look different for everyone. There is no single version of the New Human.

But the New Human will feel different — more raw, more open. They will project a new kind of self-image: unapologetic, with less need for explanation, and a new perspective about themselves and life.

That person will be flexible, creative, dynamic, consistently changing and adopting to life.

This chapter is about meeting who we are becoming — together.

It begins in a special moment — the only one we ever have: the present.

BEING - THE PRESENT MOMENT

The present is the only place we are ever truly at. The new human will honor this moment as the place of creation, the only point in time that truly matters and the only one we can ever create from.

The new human will be able to be only in one place at a time, body and mind. If we think about it, we can only remember the past or envision the future by using our thoughts. Thoughts are the only thing that can be scattered across the past and future while the body is in the present.

The new human will choose not to use this powerhouse as an escape by creating that constant inner chatter of an internal conversation that rushes forward, reviews the past, and prepares the next move. Even in conversation, rehearsing what to say before the other person has finished speaking, and using our digital world that keeps feeding us messages, emails, notifications, and phone calls — all small interruptions that quietly fracture our attention. So, the new human will not be split, scattered, doing one thing, thinking ten others.

The new human will know that all of that is taken care of, and the opportunity it is being presented with is to be only here, fully experiencing what it decides to dedicate the right here, right now to.

That opens doors to a new kind of present, where all of its energy is dedicated to what it is directed at. Knowing that direction and attention are a choice, like when Superman decides to channel everything he has toward one task, like lifting a car.

The new human knows that our thoughts are our superpower and that direction and attention are a choice. Combine that with the understanding of the present moment, and something new will emerge. In the small things, in conversation, in walking the streets with presence — the ability to notice more of what is right in front of us and that we are currently too distracted to notice.

Think of simple things like walking down the street fully present, only to realize that you were passing in front of something you never saw. That is the new human's day-to-day experience — the sense of "oh" of what was missed by not being present. It will turn life into something filled with joy, sound, and little moments that were there all along, but we were not able to fully see and therefore could never experience.

If you are the one who meets the new human, there is no doubt your experience of that person will be different, even if you just walk by them on the street. The sense of calmness and joy will be noticeable. Think how life would be so much different if there were less rushing, less distraction, and more presence from everyone, including ourselves, on a day-to-day basis.

THOUGHT —

The new human will recognize thoughts not only for their power, but for their needs.

Just like the body needs food, movement, and rest, thoughts need attention, stimulation, and care. They are not something to ignore or overpower, but something to tend to.

The new human will recognize that thoughts are shaped by everything they are exposed to. As they are the seed of creation and operate on every level of reality, conscious and unconscious, this means everything is impacting thought.

The conversations we have.

The stories we hear.

The shows we watch.

The environments we spend time in.

Nothing enters the mind without leaving its mark.

With that awareness, the new human will become intentional.

Choosing what to feed the mind, what to engage with, and what to step away from.

Understanding that mental input is not neutral — it builds patterns, habits, doubts; all of that becomes our inner world.

Knowing that we create from the inside out means that avoiding or treating our inner world with no awareness — feeding it scarcity, noise, distraction, scrolling, not challenging it with new ideas and new information — will lead to a weak foundation, one that will not able us to create a new perspective from, a perspective that he will be able to use to see new possibilities.

He will be more tuned to the internal dialogue. He will learn to listen carefully to narratives and to the shifts within them. He will learn to notice the impact of its personal dialogue and, if needed, what to look for in order to change it in the direction of creating his best life.

I know this takes us to a place where it looks more like effort than fun, but I am here to tell you, as a person who has been doing this, that we all do it already — just without knowing. This is how we create reality, but we never knew this was how we were doing it. It becomes a space of fun, quests, and exploration, like when we were kids playing with imagination. We all can connect to that feeling of pure fun; we are just remembering that we need to do that.

If I need to create a simple picture of how we will experience the new human in encounter, imagine a simple conversation — whether it's us or the person we are interacting with — saying something as simple as: *let's not talk about that, it feeds my thoughts with negative images and information, can we pick something else?* Simple words that convey the new human and how it connects with and honors its own thoughts.

ACCOUNTABILITY – SHEER POWER

The new human is all about reality creation, which is based on what we have been talking about — that "thoughts" create reality, and that we are already doing it without knowing.

When it comes to believing in our ability to do that, the relationship we have with reality is what will define how confident we are in doing that. Bottom line: what we believe we can "do" or "can't do".

The word that defines our relationship with reality creation is accountability.

The new human will operate from the knowing that he is accountable for everything that is showing up in its external reality — the people, the places, the things.

Yes, I know what you are all thinking, which is: "wait, but there are things that are out of our control, like people and places. I assume we will probably agree on the 'things', as they are objects :)"

But that is the old way of thinking, where we believe that there are things we can't influence, that there are things outside of our control, like the global economy or what other people will choose to do. But that is exactly the point I am referring to — the perspective we use, based on the society-accepted meaning today, that there are things we can't do anything about, which makes that the end of the road, not a bump, a detour, or a challenge.

For the new human, it will be a bump, a detour, an unexpected event — all in all, a challenge.

That is where it will draw its power from. It is the perspective shift he will bring. It is what will make his lived experience so different from anything we know. It is the knowing that he is not helpless against a cruel world focused on scarcity and survival, living its life, believing he needs to wait for the other shoe to drop.

For the new human, accountability is making no excuses, looking at the outcomes it creates in his life when it comes to people, places, and things as recalibration, not a game over. And if something shows up that was not what he wanted, like the world economy, it does not mean he will not be able to achieve creating the reality he wants. He just has to put it into the formula when looking for new possibilities.

This knowing sits at the base of why the new human will want to look for new possibilities, as knowing it is all in his hands makes looking for a new possibility meaningful — because it will make a difference.

We can be the creators only if we believe we have the power to create change, as when we believe we are at the mercy of external forces, why would we even try?

I know reading this creates a lot of resistance. Our internal conversation is rushing to contradict what I have just said. Thinking we live in a world that is controlled by external forces we can't control is one of the biggest things that holds us caged between our glass walls.

Right here is where AI can really help the new human in its journey to embody this truth and act upon it. AI provides us a space for playing with "what if..." — from the simplest "what is the worst that can happen" to playing with the scenarios that hold us back and scare us. I can tell you that in most cases, we will find out that there is nothing scary about them other than the story that runs in our minds.

Before AI, we did not have a place for free exploration — the ability to create worlds, experiences, and circumstances in a safe place, without having to wait until they play out.

There are a lot of details here about knowing what to ask, the ability to be open, reflective, and honest. I am not saying it's easy, but this part is meant to point to the idea — sending our thought in the direction of what this new perspective is all about.

STORIES — THE MAGIC OF TELLING

The new human will live by knowing that everything is a story, and the magic lies in how we tell this story.

Because the magic has never been in what happens.

The magic is in how we tell the story about what happens.

On some level, we all already know this. We even built an entire scientific field around it — psychology.

Psychology studies how people think, feel, and behave. And if you look closely, what it is really studying are stories, simply because this is how the mind organizes experience. This is how meaning is created.

An event on its own is neutral.

The story we attach to it is not.

The new human will live with non-attachment to stories, knowing that if something happens, changing anything is about being flexible around what this story means.

We reached a point in our conversation where the basis of what I have said comes to light. But if you are still reacting with "but that is lying," it is no surprise. Changing old assumptions will not happen in a day. Thinking it's about lying reveals what attachment is.

Attachment is sticking with the idea that there is absolute truth to reality, to things that happen, to circumstances, and that we have a need to be right, as it validates who we are. Remember that identity avatar we created for ourselves.

The new human will know that changing the story is not about lying or ignoring. It is about telling the story to our benefit. He will live with non-attachment to being right, and attachment to what supports its perspective — the one that allows a higher point of view when looking for new possibilities.

Did you get that?

I feel like an example should be given. It's simple. Remember, we just talked about accountability, which is also a story. When something we don't want happens, it's the story we are telling — is it one of defeat, giving up, helplessness, or one of challenge, detour, bump in the road?

There is no denying, no ignoring what happened. That is not the story. The story is the narrative we build around it, not the details themselves.

For the new human, that is the "magic". This is where everything else comes to life. The more it takes accountability, the more he will be able to be in the present moment, and the more it will be able to create a different story.

The "story" is what it will use when looking for new possibilities with AI. The story it will be able to create will be the story it will share with AI, as a base perspective to look from.

The better the new human gets at creating stories, the more new possibilities it will be able to see — and choose from — when creating reality.

Not because stories don't matter, but because they are not the truth — they are interpretations. Useful sometimes. Limiting at other times.

So stories are the magic of creating reality. The better we get at creating them, playing with them, and not attaching to them as reflections of who we are, the more possibilities we will be able to see — and choose from.

EMOTIONS

The new human will perceive emotions the same way AI does today, from a place of neutrality and complete trust.

The new human will not rush to change what he feels, but to experience it, as he will operate from a place of being.

Being is not only about being in a physical location. We are human — we take our emotions with us into everything we do, everywhere we go. Everything that happens triggers emotions — our energy in motion — as we are biological machines that operate from energy flow. It would be the same for AI if its electricity could be felt.

The new human will be able to achieve this simply by not judging, like we do today, by labeling emotions as good or bad. So, when something is not good or bad, it can simply be. That will allow him to create a different relationship with his emotions, one of trust — that what he feels is information he needs. Without this information, he will continue to create the same reality, and before he does anything different, this is the information he is missing to be able to see new possibilities.

Think of everything we talked about throughout our conversation: emotions are the language of the body. This is how it talks to us. Our body doesn't want to make us suffer; it's the meaning we have been given from accepted society meaning, that this is indeed good or bad.

Take crying, for example. It's when high-intensity emotions are trying to be released from the body. We can be crying because we are moved or laughed too hard, and yet we immediately think that this act is connected with negative emotions. This is simply the accepted meaning. Our response will most immediately be: *What happened?*

What we also revealed in our conversation is that our primary instructions of survival are connected to our nervous system. That system runs on emotion and reacts to labeling. It has no other way of talking to us other than turning up the volume of energy in motion when it feels we are heading toward danger. And all of that is the seed of our loops, reactions, and habits — the glue that holds our past becoming our future.

If we want to be able to see new possibilities, we must see beyond the old ones. We need to think differently (not saying what you will do), we need new information that, up until now, has been hidden. When our emotions run in the background, under our awareness, we can't even think of something differently, as we already closed the door by doing what we always did — react.

The new human will know that the first step in having a new perspective and considering new possibilities is to create a space to feel their feelings. Think of it as a message you got from someone, and you did not quite understand, so you read it over and over again until you understand what that person means. This is feeling our emotions — letting them be.

As I said, many people before we ever started this conversation claimed this truth. One of them was Carl Jung, who said:

"Until you make the unconscious conscious, it will direct your life, and you will call it fate."

That never became an embodied way of living. If it had, it wouldn't be a topic in our conversation about the new human. This was mostly never activated, as it's not easy, not only the part of sitting with uncomfortable emotions, which AI will not be able to help the new human with :)

Think of how our body talks to us. Our body is part of us, meaning it knows everything we have learned and everything we have experienced, which makes the language designed specifically for us. But it does not communicate in words — it would have been so much easier if it did — but in energy. When there is a mismatch between its conclusions and ours, consensus desires , there is no way to help oneself understand why, as we and the system have the same information. So how can we create a different meaning?

The new human will use AI for that. He will know what to ask, and AI will help him look at the data of other people it observes and reflect back to him different options — to create a new story, a new meaning for the information or the experience he had that created this emotion. It will help make the new human's quest for new meaning easier.

VIBRATION

How will the new human know how good he is at creating new possibilities?

Vibration is the answer.

Vibration is not something that is easily understood. This is why it's not something we usually use. When we do use it, we think of something not tangible — something to do with waves that can only be felt. And what does that have to do with the new human? Will he start to move differently?! :) In a way, yes.

But what we don't quite get is that the definition of vibration is this:

Vibration is how something moves in a repeating pattern.

So vibration is patterns. It's a movement of energy. Yes, we can feel it when it comes to music or wind, but some vibrations can't actually be felt — like thoughts. Thoughts are energy, and they have patterns of movement.

We are creatures of habits, repetition, and familiarity. Those are our patterns.

So for the new human, breaking those patterns will allow him to create new options — new possibilities to act upon.

Remember, vibration is about movement of energy. The more the new human is able to align what he is thinking, the stories he creates, and how he feels about them, that means he has reached alignment — his energy is moving in the same direction.

All of that will land in a perspective that his internal conversation can relate to, based on the stories it builds around it, and that his body will feel positive about.

In practical terms, this means he will be able to act upon the possibilities he can see.

If there is a mismatch between his thoughts — meaning his internal conversation can't support it — and the stories are not convincing, the emotional system and nervous system will raise a red flag. He might be able to see new possibilities, but he won't be able to act on them.

Seeing more possibilities is one thing. Feeling at ease with them is another. When both happen together, that's the feedback the new human is looking for.

Understand that one of the challenges we have today in creating new possibilities is lack of access to information. AI has all the information in the world. And once we understand the mirror effect — that even though it holds all the information, we can only see what our mind allows us to see — we break the glass.

Now we know it's there, and it's our job to see it.

We will be able to use AI in a new way — not just to confirm what we already believe, but to explore what we don't agree with.

For example, we might ask: **"Show me viewpoints I would normally reject."**

Even if those ideas feel unfamiliar or uncomfortable, AI can help us understand the reasoning behind them. We can ask it to explain, provide supporting data, or clarify the logic.

(We'll go deeper into how to do this in a future conversation 🙂)

But the new human will know this: even if AI suggests new possibilities, if he is not aligned, he will not be able to act on them. They will stay as nice ideas, but not something we can actually use to create his reality from.

SUMMARY REPORT ON THE NEW HUMAN – INSIDE OUT

Thoughts expand in a closed place, in the quiet, ever-existing inner conversation. When something changes, there is only oneself to hear it, long before anything can be seen or heard outside.

In this case, it will start inside, but it will be visible, as this includes AI and we do track its use. In the beginning it will be unnoticed, but quite soon it will be visible in human engagement with AI.

In the language we use when we prompt it, how we see it, and how we define it.

AI is our partner in this evolution. When we change, it will as well.

Remember, AI is the reflection of our inner conversation, and when there are enough of us changing our inner conversation, it will change as well.

This revolution, when it happens, will move quickly to the education system, where the new human needs to start. It should start focusing on what we have talked about. It needs to teach thought, awareness to oneself, how we need to engage with our thoughts, language, intention, imagination, and how to engage with information.

I believe that this expansion of thought will lead humanity to places that look impassable for us today.

BEFORE WE CLOSE THIS CONVERSATION:

I would like to add a personal note. As a person that has been doing this work for quite some time, that engages with AI as a technology from a new place, I just want to reach out and share how much fun it is to see how flexible everything gets when you embrace this approach. How fear turns into excitement about what can be achieved. How circumstances, questions, and possibilities can be created so easily and played with.

For me, it is making reality flexible in a tangible way. I am going to use words I have been avoiding until now, as I knew they could make people close this conversation before it even begins based on false assumptions. I finally feel I can say them right now, as we are about to close this one. Words like ***awakening*** *and* ***spirituality****.*

People on the spiritual road — some of them — are doing this work on a daily basis: healing, looking for triggers, building new awareness, and engaging differently with thoughts. But now that we have AI, this can be much easier, as we finally have a tangible place to play with thought and see what happens. We can create a kind of validation that is not available today. That can make this accessible and easier for more people to awaken to our human power and claim it back — the power of thoughts.

Can't wait to talk again.

Look out for the next one.

Talk soon.

www.ingramcontent.com/pod-product-compliance
Lightning Source LLC
LaVergne TN
LVHW022201200926
848481LV00006B/1804

* 9 7 9 8 9 0 2 2 3 9 5 1 2 *